MW00444076

Mastering

Business
Finance

Authors: Neil Griffin, Don Battle, Raymond J. Lipay

Editor: Kathy A. Shipp

Editorial Director: Patrick DiDomenico

Associate Publisher: Adam Goldstein

Publisher: Phillip A. Ash

© 2011, 2005, 1996, Business Management Daily, a division of Capitol Information Group, Inc., 7600A Leesburg Pike, West Building, Suite 300, Falls Church, VA 22043-2004; www.BusinessManagementDaily.com; phone: (800) 543-2055 . All rights reserved. No part of this report may be reproduced in any form or by any means without written permission from the publisher. Printed in U.S.A.

ISBN: 9781543153828 (3rd edition)

"This publication is designed to provide accurate and authoritative information in regard to the subject matter covered. It is sold with the understanding that the publisher is not engaged in rendering legal, accounting or other professional service. If legal advice or other expert assistance is required, the services of a competent professional person should be sought."—*From a Declaration of Principles jointly adopted by a committee of the American Bar Association and a committee of publishers and associations.*

Contents

What Every Manager Should Know

No subject seems to pervade our lives as much as finance. Whether it's wrestling with your family budget or seeing if your company qualifies for a bank loan, finance looms larger than any other technical subject on a daily basis. With downsizing of companies and staffs, managers at every level are having to face financial matters in ever-greater proportions today. If you haven't yet been asked to scale down inventories or set up financing for departmental projects, chances are you will be soon.

In today's corporate environment, nonfinancial managers are expected to make financial decisions fast. In fact, your decision often was due "yesterday." If that's not enough pressure, the arrival of computers and cyberspace has given your competition access to more financial facts, in greater detail and more promptly, than ever before. The need to make financial decisions quickly is vital to your success. There's no time for an in-depth study of financial concepts and their meaning when your boss or your employees are expecting a yes or no answer right away.

This report is meant to strip away the fear and confusion you may experience about finance. It explains expense and capital budgets, financial analysis and cash management, and tells you how to go about raising money—all in language that's easy to understand. We explain jargon where we have to use it—and where we think that a picture would be worth a thousand words, you'll find an example or an illustration. Unlike most publications on finance, we give you not just the how but also the why of the financial process. Our goal: to bring you up to speed fast on the financial tools you need to succeed in business today.

Are You Savvy About Finance?

Before reading this report, you might find it interesting to test your current knowledge of finance. Take the following test and check your answers below.

	True	False
1. Small companies generally use "S-1" public stock registrations in their equity offerings.	❏	❏
2. Another name for "income statement" is "statement of financial changes."	❏	❏
3. "NPV" stands for "net percentage value."	❏	❏
4. Fixed costs are so named because they never change.	❏	❏
5. A current ratio gives you a good indication of a company's profitability.	❏	❏
6. Non-notification factoring rids a company of the chore of handling bookkeeping and collection payments for its receivables.	❏	❏
7. "Hurdle rate" is just another name for "current loan rate."	❏	❏
8. The payback method is a good way to measure the profitability of a capital project.	❏	❏
9. A company's first step in the budget process is to come up with a cash forecast.	❏	❏
10. "Working capital" is a fancy label for a company's cash flow.	❏	❏

Answers: All 10 questions are false.

Learning the Tools of the Trade

1

To get the big picture of the role finances play in your company, think about any major decision you or others within your company make. The decisions to hire, fire, buy, sell, start up or close down—all are financial nature. Almost any question that makes its way to your desk, and that requires a decision by you, can be put into financial terms.

In the strictest sense, the financial pro or officer in your company is still the one charged with making sure the company uses its assets to bring the greatest possible return on the money invested. To accomplish that, he or she must manage those assets, measure the need for additional assets, obtain funds to finance expansion and repay borrowed funds from profits that the assets have generated. In short, the financial officer rides herd on incoming and outgoing dollars. But, in fact, every manager has at least part of that responsibility.

It should come as no surprise to you, then, that the basic tools of the trade used to carry out these tasks begin and end in dollar signs. They are called the **balance sheet**, the **income statement** and the **statement of cash flows**. These financial statements are prepared by your accounting department or accountant on the accrual basis of accounting. According to the accrual accounting method, revenues are recorded when realized and expenses when incurred, regardless of the date when cash is actually received or disbursed.

For many nonfinancial managers, the accrual concept is confusing because most of us manage our personal finances on a cash basis. Similarly, other business financial concepts create frustration and embarrassment for managers who, often unknowingly, attempt to "simplify" things by applying personal financial practices.

For instance, most of us regard our annual income on a gross basis. Rarely do we consider depreciating personal items, such as a car for wear and tear, or amortizing less tangible goods. An examination of the balance sheet, income statement and statement of cash flows will reveal the importance of understanding the difference between business and personal finance.

The Balance Sheet

The balance sheet is a comprehensive statement of the financial picture of your company on a given date. Virtually every business prepares a balance sheet at the close of its fiscal or tax year. Many also prepare semiannual or quarterly balance sheets, and most should do so.

There are two primary sections on the balance sheet: The first one (the left side, if the two sections are shown side by side) lists your company's assets, or what it owns. The second section (right-hand side) lists liabilities, or debts, and the owner's equity in the company. Total liabilities are claims against total assets. The sum of these liabilities and equity always equals total assets (assets = liabilities + equity): hence, the name "balance sheet." The simplified balance sheet that appears on page 4 might be prepared by any manufacturing company. Other companies would have similar statements.

Sample Corporate Balance Sheet

ASSETS

Current assets

Cash and equivalents		$ 30,000
Trade accounts receivable	$80,000	
Less allowance for doubtful accounts	9,000	71,000
Inventories		
Finished goods/products	65,000	
Work in process	65,000	
Raw materials	10,000	
Supplies	5,000	145,000
Prepaid expenses		9,000
Total current assets		$255,000

Fixed assets

Furniture and fixtures	$ 9,000	
Less allowance for depreciation	4,000	5,000
Machinery and equipment	20,000	
Less allowance for depreciation	6,000	14,000
Buildings	35,000	
Less allowance for depreciation	8,000	27,000
Land		14,000
Total fixed assets		60,000

Other assets

Investments		15,000
Goodwill, patents		8,000
Total		23,000
Total assets		**$338,000**

LIABILITIES AND EQUITY

Current liabilities

Accounts payable	$ 30,000	
Notes payable	70,000	$100,000
Accrued liabilities		
Wages and salaries payable	$ 3,000	
Interest payable	1,000	4,000
Allowance for taxes		
Income tax	$14,000	
State taxes	3,000	17,000
Total current liabilities		$121,000
Long-term debt		5,000

Equity

Capital stock		$150,000
Surplus		62,000
Total equity		212,000
Total liabilities and equity		**$338,000**

Following is a description of each of the basic balance-sheet items listed, many of which will be used to construct the various financial ratios explained in Section 2.

Assets

Current assets: All cash held (primarily in bank balances or money market funds); assets that will be converted to cash in the normal course of business within one business year (trade accounts, notes receivable and inventories); plus other assets that could or will be converted within a year (marketable short-term securities, nontrade debts or debt installments owed to the company within a year). Other than cash and equivalents, current assets include inventories (in various stages of completion) and prepaid expenses (any rent, interest, insurance or taxes paid in advance).

Although the term doesn't appear in most balance sheets, the following items make up **noncurrent assets**.

Fixed assets: All property, plants and equipment (buildings, real estate, machines, transportation equipment, office equipment, furniture, etc.) used in the business. The accumulated depreciation on these items is deducted where applicable in standard accounting practice.

Other assets: All long-term investments, such as securities (stocks, bonds, mortgages), and **intangible assets**, such as goodwill, patents, trademarks and other paper assets, which may be assigned a value for determining the total sale price of the business. Intangible assets can have a significant impact on a business's ability to generate income. However, unlike a plant or equipment, they are often concepts or legal entitlements.

Total assets: The sum of the current, fixed and other assets listed above.

Liabilities and Equity

Current liabilities: Outstanding trade debts and obligations (trade accounts payable, short-term notes and loans payable, current installments due on long-term debts, etc.) that will fall due in the course of normal business within one year, plus accrued business expenses payable and accrued federal income taxes payable.

Long-term liabilities or debt: All business debts and liabilities (long-term loans, bonds, mortgages, etc.) payable more than one year beyond the date of the balance sheet.

Total liabilities: The sum of the above items.

Shareholders' equity (net worth): The par value of the corporation's common and preferred stock, plus any paid-in or accumulated capital surplus over this par value, plus any **retained earnings** for use in business. Retained earnings of the business represent the total income earned by the firm over its life less any dividends paid out to the owners. (Equity = book value of outstanding stock + capital surplus + retained earnings)

Total liabilities and equity: The sum of the above two groups, which by definition is also equal to the total assets of the business.

The Income Statement

The income statement (also called the earnings report or profit-and-loss statement) reflects the results of operation over a period of time, in contrast to the balance sheet's snapshot view of the company's financial condition at a given instant. Again, every business must prepare an annual income statement for tax, legal and other purposes; nevertheless, semiannual, quarterly or even monthly statements can be extremely useful. The items included in the simplified income statement on page 6 will often be needed to create the financial ratios used in your analysis and covered in the next section. Briefly, here is a description of the items contained in a company's income statement:

Sample Income Statement

Gross sales or revenues	$ 605,000
Returns, discounts and allowances	30,000
Net sales or revenues	575,000
Cost of sales or goods sold	470,000
Gross margin or operating profit	$ 105,000
Selling and administrative costs	60,000
Depreciation	5,000
Net operating profit	$ 40,000
Interest income or nonoperating income	10,000
Interest expense or nonoperating expense	3,000
Net profit before taxes	$ 47,000
Provision for federal income taxes	10,000
Net profit after taxes	$ 37,000

Gross sales or revenues: The actual total dollars billed for goods sold or services provided, before returns, discounts and allowances granted. Sales income and accounts receivable determine this first line item.

Net sales or revenues: Gross sales minus returns, discounts and allowances.

Cost of goods sold: The amounts paid for the purchased materials, components and finished products; direct payroll, operating overhead; and other costs of acquiring or producing the products or services and making them available for sale. This line item often appears as **less cost of goods sold**.

Gross profit: The difference between net sales or revenues and the cost of the products or services sold. This represents the amount of money left to sell the product and perform the day-to-day operations of the business.

Selling and administrative costs: Selling costs include salespersons' salaries and commissions, travel and entertainment expenses, sales promotion and advertising costs. Administrative costs include office salaries and expenses, executive salaries and other current support expenses that can't be allocated to production or sales departments.

Depreciation: The costs of plant assets (or fixed assets: property, plant and equipment) are written off as expenses over their anticipated useful life. Not all fixed assets are depreciated, however. For instance, the value of land tends to appreciate in value because it does not typically wear out. There are various depreciation techniques an accountant can use. The simplest and most commonly used method in U.S. businesses is called the **straight-line method of depreciation**, which allows you to depreciate the same amount of expense each year of the estimated useful life of the asset. For example, an asset with a value of $10,000 and a useful life of 10 years will have an annual $1,000 depreciation expense each year.

Net operating profit: Gross profit, less selling costs and administrative overhead. This line item represents the profit generated by the normal operations of the business.

Nonoperating income: Interest and dividends received on investments, gains on the disposition of capital assets, etc.

Nonoperating expenses: Interest paid on long-term debts, losses on sales of capital assets, etc.

Net profit before taxes: Net operating profit, plus any nonoperating income and minus any nonoperating expenses.

Provision for federal income taxes: The estimated amount to be paid on operating earnings for the period, not the amount of taxes paid during the period.

Net profit (or income) after taxes: The final "bottom line" profit cleared by the business from all sources during the period covered by the statement. Using this vital figure, stockholders can evaluate management, investors can decide on whether to purchase the company's stock, and creditors can measure the riskiness of a loan.

The Statement of Cash Flows

The statement of cash flows, which shows the movement of cash through a business, presents the cash receipts and cash payments of a company over a period of time. It complements the income statement by providing information on a company's liquidity and financial flexibility. It also explains the change of cash and cash equivalents during a period. (Cash equivalents are short-term, highly liquid investments that are readily convertible to cash amounts, such as short-term Treasury bills, commercial paper and money market funds.) In similar fashion to the balance sheet and the income statement, the statement of cash flows must be prepared annually by every business but may also be done semiannually or quarterly.

Note: Effective for annual financial statements for fiscal years ending after July 15, 1988, the statement of cash flows supersedes the statement of changes in financial position, which the Financial Accounting and Standards Board (FASB) formerly required. Not-for-profits, however, are not required to make the switch-over.

By using the statement of cash flows in conjunction with information provided by the balance sheet and the income statement, company owners, creditors and others who use financial statements can assess a company's ability to generate future net cash inflows, meet debt obligations and pay dividends. The statement should also help in assessing a company's need for future external financing, as well as the effects of both cash and noncash investing and financing activities on a company's financial position.

The statement of cash flows is classified by operating, investing and financing activities. *(See sample statement on page 8.)* Briefly, these are the items contained in a company's statement of cash flows:

Operating Activities:
Cash received from:
- Sale of goods or services.
- Collections or sales of receivables that arise from the sales of goods and services.
- Interest on loans and bonds.
- Dividends on equity securities.
- Insurance and lawsuit settlements.
- Refunds from suppliers.

Cash paid to:
- Acquisition of materials for inventory or manufacturing products, or for goods for resale, including payments on trade accounts and notes payable to suppliers.
- Creditors for interest.
- Employees for compensation.
- Governmental agencies for taxes, duties, fees, fines or penalties.
- Customers for refunds.
- Lawsuit settlements.
- Charities for contributions.

Investing Activities:
Cash received from:
- Sales of property, plant, equipment and other productive assets.
- Sales of a business unit such as a branch, division or subsidiary.
- Collections of principal on debt instruments of other companies.
- Sale of loans.

Cash paid to:
- Acquire property, plant, equipment and other productive assets.
- Acquire another business.
- Make loans to and/or purchase loans from another company.
- Acquire debt or equity investments in other companies.

Financing Activities:

Cash received from:

- Issuing equity instruments, such as stock in the company.
- Issuing bonds, mortgages, notes and other forms of short-term or long-term borrowing.

Cash paid to:
- Owners of the company in the form of dividends or other distributions.
- Repayment of amounts borrowed on short-term and long-term debt.

Sample Statement of Cash Flows

Cash flows from operating activities

Cash received from customers	$110,000	
Cash paid to suppliers and employees	(90,000)	
Interest received	8,000	
Interest paid	(6,000)	
Income taxes paid	(9,000)	
Net cash provided by operating activities		$13,000

Cash flows from investing activities

Proceeds from sale of plant	$70,000	
Purchase of equipment	(10,000)	
Net cash provided by investing activities		$60,000

Cash flows from financing activities

Principal payments on notes	($40,000)	
Dividends paid	(15,000)	
Net cash used in financing activities		($55,000)
Net increase in cash and equivalents		18,000
Cash and equivalents at beginning of year		12,000
Cash and equivalents at end of year		$30,000

Reconciliation of net profit to net cash provided by operating activities:

Net profit after taxes		$37,000

Adjustments to reconcile net profit after taxes to net cash provided by operating activities:

Depreciation		2,000
Gain on sale of plant		(11,000)
Increase in trade accounts receivable		(7,000)
Increase in inventory		(10,000)
Decrease in accounts and notes payable		5,000
Increase in interest and taxes payable		(3,000)
Net cash provided by operating activities		$13,000

The most straightforward way to present operating activities in a statement of cash flows is the direct method, which reports major classes of operating cash receipts and payments. Under this method, a separate schedule is presented with the statement of cash flows that reconciles net profit and net cash flow from operating activities. In effect, this **reconciliation** is a conversion of net profit from the accrual to the cash basis of accounting.

➤ **Observation:** You'll find the balance sheet, the income statement and the statement of cash flows in a company's annual report. In most annual reports these financial statements are presented on a comparative basis: that is, the current year along with one or more prior years. Use the figures in these statements to analyze your own company as well as your competition, to forecast the financial outcome for your entire business or department project, and to make a variety of other essential business decisions. In short, these reports are three of the businessperson's most important tools.

How the Financial Pros Use These Tools

2

Now that you are aware of the mechanics of a balance sheet, an income statement and a statement of cash flows, your work is not over yet. Keep in mind that although the figures in those reports are important, they don't, in and of themselves, tell you how your company is doing compared with others in your industry, whether it has staying power in our highly competitive world or what weaknesses it should be correcting from within. In short, those reports alone do not tell you whether the company is financially healthy.

To determine the financial state of your company, you have to turn to three major conditions within your company that you, as a manager, can help control or change:

- **Liquidity**, which is simply the ability to generate enough cash to pay your bills and expenses on time.
- **Leverage**, which is the relationship between your company's total liabilities and equity. Your firm is said to be highly leveraged when it has a lot of debt in relation to equity. In some instances, carrying a lot of debt can be advantageous. At other times, it can be injurious to a company's health. Those pros and cons will be discussed later in this section.
- **Profitability**, which is simply whether your company ends up with any money after all your expenses, including taxes, have been paid. Profitability, in other words, is reflected in the "bottom line" of your income statement and determines whether you should be in business at all.

Troubleshooting With Ratio Analysis

Financial analysts examine the liquidity, leverage, profitability and other vital aspects of a firm by using the figures in the company's financial statements to form special relationships or ratios. These ratios are the most common source of information they use to assess the performance of a business. They can relate any aspect of your business to any other area, such as sales to profits, or profits to assets. Most important, because they are so widely used and reported, it is possible to compare ratios for your own business with the average for your industry, or for groups of companies within your industry.

Sometimes, however, ratio analysis can lead you astray if you are not aware of its limitations. First, ratio analysis is geared toward giving you insights rather than hard business data. As such, it can point the way to possible trouble spots, but you will need further verification when you get there. For instance, a downturn in your operating profit margin might point out an operating bottleneck, but you will need to investigate further to isolate the problem. Moreover, ratios deal with historical data, which may or may not be relevant to current economic trends or company needs. For this reason, it is always wise to confirm that a trend indicated by a ratio analysis is, in fact, applicable to current operating conditions.

Ten Critical Ratios

Ratios come in all shapes and sizes, and are applicable to a wide range of business problems. More than 150 financial ratios are currently in use. For our purposes, we have chosen 10 ratios, each addressing a specific potential problem area and derived from the balance sheet and/or income statement. These 10 critical ratios are basic analytical tools for most businesses. The following list details their components and principal significance:

1. **Current ratio:** Total current assets, divided by total current liabilities at the same point in time. The standard test measure of the relative adequacy of working capital, or of the **liquidity** of the business. **Recommendation:** Generally, healthy firms aim for a 2 to 1 current ratio, which means they have $2 in current assets for every $1 of current liabilities.

2. **Debt/equity:** Total current and long-term liabilities divided by average shareholders' equity. Measures the **leverage**, or the extent to which the business depends on borrowed capital, and whether creditors or the owners have a larger interest in the enterprise. **Recommendation:** As a general rule, this ratio should equal roughly .6.

3. **Return on equity:** Net profit for the period, divided by average shareholders' equity for the period. This is the true return on the net investment of the owners' capital tied up in business, and the most basic ratio in the family of **return on investment (ROI)** ratios. This ratio, along with ratio No. 4, measures the third condition you're looking at in analyzing a company: **profitability**. **Recommendation:** This figure should be .14 or higher, which means a company should return at least 14 percent to begin satisfying its investors.

4. **Return on assets:** Net operating profit for the period, divided by average total tangible assets for the period. This is another ratio used to measure the ROI of the total capital being used in the business.

5. **Net profit margin:** Net profit divided by net sales for the same period. This key measure reflects the successful or unsuccessful interaction of sales efforts, prices and costs over the period. **Recommendation:** Use this ratio to compare your figures with those of other companies in your industry, or to compare net profit on sales for individual products or product lines. As a manager, you can then recommend which products should be promoted or dropped.
   Note: Ratios 6 through 9 are generally referred to as **operating ratios**. They are most useful when making historical comparisons within the company or with others in your industry.

6. **Receivables turnover:** Credit sales divided by average accounts receivable for the entire period. A measure of relative health of outstanding receivables, in that the higher the ratio, the faster accounts are being paid up.

7. **Inventory turnover:** Cost of goods sold divided by average inventory for the period. This is a yardstick to measure the relative adequacy of inventories, or the speed with which inventories are turned over. If the ratio keeps decreasing, your customer's inventories are probably excessive and draining needed cash. If the ratio suddenly rises, inventories may be too low and thus may endanger production schedules.

8. **Fixed-asset turnover:** Net sales divided by gross plant and equipment (before depreciation deduction) for the period. This is an index of the amount of fixed capital required to produce each sales dollar. It is used to determine whether you're using your fixed assets efficiently.

9. **Total asset turnover:** Net sales divided by average total tangible assets for the period. A measure of the effective employment of the total assets of the business.

10. **Equity turnover:** Net sales divided by average shareholders' equity for the period. This is the basic measure for comparing sales produced by the owners' net investment with that of other companies, periods or industries. The ratio indicates the turnover of investment capital, or how hard the invested capital is working. There isn't any general norm for this ratio; each line of business sets its own.

Now let's take a look at the practical applications of some of these and other ratios by asking the following questions:

Does your firm have enough cash to pay its bills?

Lack of cash can be a major problem simply because cash inflow is uncertain, while the required cash outflow is constant and necessary to maintain regular business operations. For that reason, a business must try to maintain certain levels of cash to pay its bills by maintaining a safe **current ratio**. In other words, it keeps an eye on its liquidity.

Example: In our sample balance sheet *(see page 4)*, the current ratio would be:

$$\frac{\text{Current assets (\$255,000)}}{\text{Current liabilities (\$121,000)}} = 2.1$$

Our sample company seems to have adequate liquidity.

To leverage or not to leverage?

A highly leveraged company has its pros and cons. Many entrepreneurs seek out a leveraged firm because they believe they can earn enough with a company both to pay the interest on debt and make a good return. In other words, leverage can increase profits.

In bad times, a highly leveraged firm can react the same way as an individual drowning in debt. Interest payments become hard to meet, and creditors begin closing in for the kill. For that reason, bankers and management people pay close attention to the debt/equity ratio to see if there's any undue drain on funds.

Example: Again in our sample balance sheet:

$$\frac{\text{Total liabilities (\$126,000)}}{\text{Shareholders' equity (\$212,000)}} = .59$$

Again, our sample company seems to be sitting pretty!

How profitable is your firm?

Depending on how much it wants to make, every company has its own norm for what the **return on equity** ratio should be. We used 14 percent as a minimum. Others, however, say that the return should at least match the going rate for Treasury bills, or a firm might be better off using the capital invested in the firm for some other purpose.

Example: For this ratio, we turn both to our balance sheet for the equity figure and to the income statement *(see page 6)* for the net income figure:

$$\frac{\text{Net income (\$37,000)}}{\text{Equity (\$212,000)}} = 17\%$$

It looks like our sample financial statements indicate a very healthy company.

Should you provide credit to a customer?

Often, you will need information from a customer to be able to answer this question. When the customer provides a balance sheet or income statement, you need to know what to look for. Practically speaking, the income statement is likely to be out of date and won't represent the company's current financial affairs. Most companies prepare income statements only once or twice each year, but monthly balance sheets are common.

If you obtain an up-to-date income statement, it will not require much additional work to come up with a complete picture of the company's current state of affairs. Luckily, even without a current income statement, you can learn much from the balance sheet by using ratio analysis. As you can see, most ratio analysis requires only basic math skills.

From our list of 10 critical ratios, use the current ratio to determine whether the customer is liquid enough to pay off debts, and use the return on equity ratio to see whether the customer is profitable. Use the inventory turnover ratio to determine if the customer will be able to meet your production schedules. When using ratios that require sales figures, those for the latest year available will suffice. In addition, the following ratios are important:

- **Current liabilities to net worth:** how much of the funds invested by your customers would be needed to pay off all short-term obligations. The lower the ratio, the better. Normally, you should shy away from a firm with a ratio of 66 percent or higher.
- **Short-term debt coverage:** current assets divided by short-term debt. This ratio is a variation of the current ratio, with the emphasis on short-term debt (debt due within one year). If your customer has $2 of current assets to cover each $1 of debt, you are safe. A 1:1 ratio will suffice if the current assets are easily converted into cash.
- **Average collection period:** accounts receivable divided by credit sales times 365. This ratio will give you a good idea of how fast your customer is collecting its bills. Usually, 35–45 days is considered normal. Anything over 50 days may indicate sizable uncollectible accounts and should give you just cause for concern.

Example: If a company with $20 million in credit sales maintained accounts receivable of $2 million, the average collection period would be 36 days ($2 million ÷ $20 million x 365 = 36.5).

▶ **Observation:** Once you decide that a new customer has the wherewithal to pay bills on time, you must determine how much credit to extend. A general rule of thumb is to fill any first order up to 10 percent of the customer's net worth and, after that, open a formal line of credit. Once approved, this line of credit should be exceeded only with top management's approval.

Answering Some Difficult Financial Questions

3

Ratio analysis can be very helpful in pinpointing operating inefficiencies within your company. But to understand **how** you can use ratios to spot problems, you must first know the right questions to ask. In this section we address some of the important financial questions that all managers should be asking.

A Question of Profit Margins

Has profit growth kept pace with sales growth in recent years? If not, have some markets been more responsible than others for the lag?

Many managers wrongly believe that as a company grows and matures, profits always increase at a slower rate than sales, even as both continue to expand. This is called the principle of diminishing returns on added volume. However, this principle is often untrue. Consider the following example.

A manufacturer of small parts and components for finished products found that economies of scale and other growth factors were no longer bringing satisfactory profit growth. Rather, it appeared that increased sales volume had come partly from its entry into new markets that were more competitive, more expensive to promote and serve, and generally less profitable.

One of the first analytical figures the top managers turned to was the familiar **net profit margin**, on a market-by-market basis. To begin, the firm's sales analyst produced reports showing net profit margins on sales by markets for each of the last three years. These reports showed all the costs associated with getting the sale and subtracted them out of the gross sales figure. These results served as an important factor in decisions that later led to major changes in the company's overall marketing strategy.

A few of the industry groups, for example, had grown in both sales volume and profitability over the past few years. Several others accounted for a larger share of company sales, but revealed shrinking profit margins in this analysis as a result of substantial price discounting. For the time being, at least, little could be done about some of these industry markets because the company needed the volume they generated.

In some of the most highly competitive industry markets, however, analysis showed the company was forgoing profits without substantially improving its market position. Furthermore, the top marketing people agreed that there was little likelihood of changing this situation for the better in the near future. Management decided to deemphasize sales efforts in these markets, except at full-profit pricing. Although sales volume fell off, the sales efforts were retargeted to more profitable industry sectors. It was not long before the growth trend for overall net profit reversed its decline and slowly began to improve.

Sometimes a company is unable to break down all its selling and administrative costs by market segment or similar criteria. One alternative is simply to allocate these costs in proportion to the sales volume in the market segment to which they are related. This, in effect, assumes that selling costs are more or less uniform in the various markets, which may not be the case.

Often, you can make a useful analysis by dividing gross profit, instead of net operating profit, by net sales. This **gross profit margin** is widely used in retailing and other nonmanufacturing industries.

Still another option, when selling and administrative costs cannot be fully allocated, is to calculate the ratio of **gross profit to cost of goods sold** in addition to, or even instead of, the above ratios. This ratio can be particularly useful in fields where bidding prices are calculated and quoted on contracts on the basis of production cost estimates. Comparisons over time—between markets or even between customers—can reveal precisely to what degree profit sacrifices are being made, in terms of the lower profit return on production outlays, to obtain volume.

➤ **Observation:** In this and other internal ratio analyses involving profits, the income statement item to start with is the net operating profit, rather than the broader net profit before (or after) taxes. First, federal income tax rates change from year to year and with the size of company profits, so using after-tax profits for internal purposes would merely introduce a complicating factor, not to mention the need to allocate one more item. Second, because the various internal comparisons being made are always between operating parts of the business, the inclusion of any nonoperating income or expense would distort the results. In some lines of business, accountants and industry groups use the profit concept of "earnings before interest and taxes" (EBIT), which is roughly the same as net operating profit plus depreciation. This figure eliminates both federal income taxes and interest earned or paid on long-term investments and debts.

RMA's *Annual Statement Studies*

A good way to compare your company's ratios with other companies' is to obtain a copy of the Risk Management Association (RMA) *Annual Statement Studies*. These studies are culled from more than 86,000 financial statements of bank borrowers reviewed by RMA, a national organization of bank lending officers, and they include information on closely held companies and public corporations.

The data is classified into two main sections: The first contains composite balance sheet and income statement comparisons for each of 355 industries for the past five years. The second section contains 17 commonly used ratios, presented as medians and quartiles, for most of the industries. With that information, a manager can zero in very quickly on where a company stands. For further information, go to www.rmahq.org.

A Question of Working Capital

Do you have enough working capital to take advantage of investment opportunities? If not, are some of your departments more to blame and need more tightening up than others?

The dollar difference between any business's current assets and its current liabilities is aptly called **working capital**. This is the amount of ready cash and readily convertible assets that you can put to work as needed, without leaving the company in a dangerously exposed financial position. Working capital is what enables your firm to take advantage of special deals, earn cash discounts, borrow short-term funds more advantageously or capitalize on similar profit opportunities. It also enables the company to meet its trade obligations and debt installments on time. The ratio most commonly used to measure the adequacy of working capital is the **current ratio**.

Retail operations regularly apply the current-ratio approach for internal analyses, such as comparing the credit and financial performances of the principal departments within various stores, as well as comparing stores with each other.

To construct the current-assets component of these departmental ratios, it is a relatively simple matter to collect current data on accounts receivable (from the departmental coding on credit customers' billing) and on inventories (directly from department records). These two categories account for the largest share of total current assets found in this type of business.

For the current-liabilities component, it is equally simple for managers to break down trade accounts payable by departments by using vendor codes and merchandise category information. Some of the remaining short-term debts and expenses payable can also be allocated directly to departments with reasonable accuracy. An allocation of remaining current liabilities in proportion to departmental volume does not bias the results in any significant way.

On the current-assets side, retail operations generally apply another ratio—**receivables turnover**—to help analyze their working capital positions.

The ideal department in a retail operation is one that both contributes to working capital, reflected in a high current ratio, and has an acceptable rate of receivables turnover, indicated by a low level of outstanding receivables.

A Question of Returns

Which areas of the business will provide the best return on an increased investment of capital? How profitably is each area using the assets now assigned to it?

Where should your company spend its investment dollars? In technology? Sales development and training? Building a warehouse? Perhaps in product development? To determine a company's long-term strategy, you must know what the returns will be. We can illustrate this important concept through the following example.

A distributor of cleaning/maintenance tools and supplies operates three divisions, each aimed at a different market: (1) contract and institutional sales, which sells to large building management firms, maintenance contractors, major hospitals and similar purchasers; (2) industrial products, which sells to commercial and industrial customers largely through agents; and (3) consumer products, which markets branded and unbranded items through retail stores. The managers of all three divisions have demonstrated that they could improve their volume and market shares with infusions of capital for packaging, warehousing, delivery and other equipment. The company has decided to add to its capital investment but must decide which division should be allocated the lion's share of the funding in order to maximize the return to shareholders.

Return on shareholders' equity is what the corporation's top managers will be looking at first in this case. It's reasonable for them to assume that the division with the highest present rate of return will continue to earn the best return as it grows. And they accept the proposition that, within practical limits, all three divisions would show the same rate of sales growth in proportion to added investment.

Allocating shareholders' equity directly to the three operating divisions may seem like a difficult task. Fortunately, however, there is a practical alternative that reduces the problem to manageable proportions.

Constructing three divisional balance sheets, one can estimate shareholders' equity in each division by simply subtracting liabilities from assets. Then you can calculate the three return-on-equity ratios, for both actual and future operations.

Return on assets (ROA) is another critical ratio that top managers will want to examine. Some financial experts believe that return on total assets provides the best measure of return for a company because it focuses on short-term financing. Especially in the short run, return on assets has several practical advantages over the more complex **return on equity (ROE)** ratio. First, ROA directly measures the key factor involved in the decision: an investment in tangible assets, such as storage, packaging, distribution or other equipment. Second, it avoids the necessity of considering and allocating liabilities, which in many companies may involve more uncertainty and potential error than allocating assets. Finally, it is easier for nonfinancial managers to understand and appreciate—an element that cannot be ignored in reaching an agreement.

It would be wise, however, for management to use both the return on assets ratio and the return on equity ratio in its analysis, rather than use the assets ratio as a substitute for the equity ratio. The equity ratio is the true measure of the shareholders' return on their investment in the company, and improving this return over the long run is the basic aim of any major management decisions. Moreover, the equity ratio may highlight certain important results of an actual decision that the asset ratio would not pick up at all.

One element taken into account in the equity ratio, for example, will be the differing effects of various asset investment decisions on the company's liabilities over time. If one division would use its added investment for a short-lived delivery fleet, while another would use it for added warehousing space, the immediate effects on the asset ratio would be very similar. The effects over a few years on both assets and liabilities, and therefore on the equity ratio, however, could be very different. The latter, of course, would be the more accurate measure of prospective rates of return on the alternative investment proposals.

A Question of Asset Management

Have recent volume gains been achieved at the price of a disproportionate tie-up of available assets? For example, have the costs of expanding operations into new territories been worth it?

In any business—manufacturing, distribution or services—it takes an investment of the owners' capital in the business assets to produce sales or revenues. In capital-intensive manufacturing industries especially, the amount of assets required for each sales dollar can be one of the most critical elements in the company's success or failure. Knowing just where the company's assets are being used most and least effectively to create sales, therefore, is of vital concern to management.

Example: A regional manufacturer of plumbing and heating systems made a basic decision to set up assembly facilities progressively in new locations, rather than extend its shipping range from its original location. The management believed this was the best path to geographical expansion of its marketing area. To date, one undesirable result has been a steady decline in the dollars of sales produced by each dollar of company assets, as the total investment in plant and equipment has grown. Top managers have therefore begun a complete review of the original decision on territorial expansion.

One of the most critical numbers to analyze is the **total asset turnover** (net sales divided by total tangible assets) and **equity turnover** (net sales divided by total shareholders' equity). A third ratio that will be particularly useful in the analysis is **fixed-asset turnover** (net sales divided by gross plant and equipment), which measures how efficiently facilities are used to produce sales.

The figures common to all three of these turnover ratios, for the company's purposes, are the sales dollars produced by each of its territorial plants, as well as by the home plant. Fortunately, it is a simple matter to obtain the needed dollar sales volume information for each plant from shipping records checked against customer billings. The other figures involved in making up each ratio are, respectively, tangible assets, shareholders' equity, and the plant and equipment (p&e) for each plant. Company records will produce the p&e figure with little, if any, adjustments required. Management will have to estimate the first two on a plant-by-plant basis by using the methods and assumptions discussed earlier.

Because the company carried out its territorial dispersion of production and assembly facilities over a period of years, management will want to look at the several territorial ratios as they have changed over, say, the last three years. This will enable it to see just how the general deterioration in company-wide ratios has developed, and to pinpoint the territorial differences in effectiveness that it expects to find.

Considering that the company's turnover ratios have definitely been slipping—and have coincided with the dispersion program—it is possible to speculate on what the analysis is likely to turn up. First, as each new assembly plant is built and brought onstream, it has undoubtedly created an initial drain on the effective use of company assets. Because the additional plants have been activated over a period of years, moreover, this drain has continued to affect turnover as the program has developed. This finding alone would be reason for changing the policy of facility dispersion.

Management will also probably find, however, that while the operating figures of some territorial plants have improved with time as they and their sales territories have become established, others have persistently lagged. In some cases, the reason may turn out to be that the size of the plant is not great enough to permit fully efficient operations. In others, it may be that not enough sales volume has developed in the territory to permit effective utilization of the new facilities.

At this point, management needs to be asking these questions: Will the plant's results improve as its sales potential is achieved? Should the plant be enlarged to make it more efficient, or should it be closed down? Can the plant be made more efficient by shifting orders to it from other territories or from the home plant?

A Question of Debt Strategy

Are we using too much—or too little—borrowed capital in our business? In either event, are we using debt financing and leasing in our various fields of operations to the extent that others do?

The words "the corporation is free of long-term debt" certainly have a solid ring in a credit report. Yet many debt-free companies have, in fact, given up valuable growth opportunities to achieve this position. And today, those that have avoided financing or leasing to acquire capital equipment and materials may have not only restricted their activities, but neglected valuable tax benefits as well.

Example: A diversified business service organization uses copying and duplicating equipment, offset printers, addressing and mailing machines, word processors and small computers in its operations. As service companies go, it is a relatively capital-intensive enterprise and must continually decide whether to own or lease new items of equipment. If the decision is to own, there is usually the further question of the relative advantage of a cash outlay versus long-term financing. At this point, company management is concerned about the overall balance between owned and leased equipment, and the more basic balance between debt and capital in the business. It would like to decide on each future equipment acquisition with these balances in mind and perhaps even change the status of some of its present equipment.

The **debt/equity ratio** is the universally accepted measure of the relationship between owner-supplied capital and that borrowed from suppliers and other creditors in any business. A high ratio compared with that of others in the same industry may be taken as a warning sign, but it may also be an indication that yours is an aggressively growing (highly leveraged) company compared with the average. Conversely, a low ratio may mean that you're in a healthy, conservative debt position, but you also haven't used the leverage of debt financing as well as you could and have missed opportunities.

Because the company competes with mailing services, contract printers, computer service bureaus and other specialized service organizations, it will want to compare its own debt/equity position with those of average companies in as many of these fields as possible. As a starting point, it has collected information from the Risk Management Association collection of ratios, as well as from Dun & Bradstreet, Inc.

To construct its own debt/equity ratios for comparison, it will be following a somewhat different course from that of the companies in the earlier examples. Instead of assigning both liabilities (debt) and assets exclusively to one field or another, it recognizes that its operations frequently overlap several fields. For each field to which it will be comparing itself, it is asking which of its assets and liabilities would be used or would exist if it were only in that field. Several asset and liability items, therefore, may be included in more than one comparison and will not always be proportionally divided among these fields.

When it has completed this exercise, management hopes to find that its debt burden, in relation to its owners' equity in the business, is no heavier than what is considered generally advisable in the major service fields in which it operates. It will also undoubtedly find, however, that compared with average companies in some of these fields, it depends significantly more, or less, on debt financing. If the reasons for these differences seem unreasonable on analysis, management intends to shift its buy-versus-lease decisions for the types of equipment involved.

A Question of Purchasing

Have our inventories, compared with sales volume, gotten out of line with those of others in our industry? Which of our products, in these terms, are showing the best and worst records, and why?

Traditionally, management has been advised that "20 percent of your products probably account for 80 percent of your inventory," so look to make the biggest cuts where most of the inventory occurs. In many cases, this approach can accomplish more harm than good and can hinder sales and deliveries of products that are among the most profitable. At the same time, it may overlook other situations that collectively account for much of the excess inventory.

Example: A manufacturer of a line of packaged housewares saw inventory values on successive reports climbing, and suspected they had gone too high. A check of inventory turnover ratios in its industry confirmed this suspicion. It began an investigation to discover why finished products were piling up, and how to correct the situation. The task was assigned to the sales manager because he was responsible for projecting sales and requisitioning output from production.

His first step was to have the available sales and inventory data organized on a detailed product basis so that he could calculate product-by-product inventory turnover ratios. It then became apparent that the suspected finished product inventories accounted for only a minor fraction of the rising inventory values reported on the balance sheet. Furthermore, because of differences in production cycles, some products generated much heavier in-process inventories than others.

Another less-expected finding was that purchased-materials stocks for certain products were a big part of the total inventory problem. Some specialized materials were in generous supply, although the products they were intended for were no longer sales leaders or were actually being phased out of the line. The inventory problem, in other words, was not only a product-by-product problem, but one that needed tackling on a stage-by-stage basis.

The sales manager's report showed inventories of the appropriate materials for each product, work-in-process and finished items at the close of all of the past four quarters. He related each of these to product sales for each quarter, to produce inventory turnover ratios in each calendar quarter. Based on his specific recommendations, the company took several actions:

- For certain products, it sharply reduced heavy and aging materials stocks. Excess items were designated for possible use in other products, as substitutes for specified materials. Those not absorbed in this way were sold off, sometimes at a gain. It also made adjustments in seasonal ordering and other purchasing practices to minimize future buildups.

- Where in-process inventories were high, the company reviewed production scheduling. Some practices that it had once adopted for convenience, and to avoid more careful scheduling, were found to be causing a significant tie-up of expensive inventories—partly finished items were being temporarily shunted aside. The **sales/in-process stock** ratios were used to zero in on these. Then changes were made to schedules, size of production runs and other practices that were adding to the inventory load.
- Finally, in a relatively few cases, stocks of products awaiting shipment were, indeed, found to be excessive. Better coordination of short-run sales projections with production orders reduced some of these. Where there were pile-ups in anticipation of seasonal needs, special preseason offers to dealers not only trimmed stocks but often resulted in a net increase in annual sales.

A Question of Stability

How well could your company withstand adversity—a sudden drop in prices or sales, or an increase in costs?

One yardstick used to answer this question is the company's **break-even point**. Expressed in sales volume, this is the point where income from sales covers total costs, both fixed and variable. Another factor that most managers watch for continuously, once the basic breakdown has been prepared, is any sign that fixed costs are rising.

Your first step, then, is to separate all costs of the company's operations into those relatively independent of the rate of operations and those that vary directly with the number of units produced. To use an obvious illustration of the first group, the cost of rent is fixed, regardless of the number of units produced. Of course, even the so-called fixed expenses may vary under conditions of extreme change (the company may dispose of or sublet part of the plant if volume falls enough). For the purposes of this rough calculation, however, we can safely ignore the possible results of such extreme changes. By contrast, direct materials costs vary almost exactly in proportion to the rate of production.

You will run into some problems in dealing with the many costs that do not clearly fall into either category—or, more correctly, contain both fixed and variable costs. An obvious example is power costs. The basic connected load charge must be borne regardless of the actual operating rate. Once a company pays the minimum, it pays for the additional consumption based on actual use. In this case, the two elements may be separated fairly easily; in others, it will be more difficult.

To illustrate, here are some guidelines for breaking down labor costs into fixed and variable categories. If sales fall off, you may be able to reduce the number of workers in a specific operation, but at what point can you also reduce the number of supervisors? If you have only one, he or she is a relatively fixed expense as long as you have even a few personnel. In the case of labor costs, you may be able to determine the minimum organization that must be retained and classify this as a fixed expense.

To take another common item, your warehousing costs contain some fixed elements (the expense of space and equipment, and at least some supervision) and some that are variable (wages of workers who may be shifted to another part of the operation if the warehouse workload falls off).

To segregate fixed and variable elements of your company's mixed costs, you will undoubtedly want to consult your company's accountant. Ask her to take each cost item for the last full year and roughly estimate the percentage that is fixed or variable within the normal range of operations. The percentages for three or four previous years and the current year can be estimated the same way, or those for the latest full year can be used after adjusting for any major differences (such as making a transition from manual work to the use of machines).

Once you have this information, calculate the break-even point in the following manner for a single year: Let's say you determine that your fixed costs (FC) are $100,000, since they don't change that much from year to year. Because you're trying to forecast your break-even point for a future time, you're not sure of your variable costs. Historically, however, they have represented approximately 80 percent of sales (variable costs divided by sales). What kind of sales do you need to break even? Your setup would look like this:

VC = variable costs (as a percentage of sales)   **S = total sales you'll need to break even**
FC = fixed costs   **P = profit**

Your break-even formula is: **P = S – (FC + VC)**
Therefore, your formula would be: **P = S – ($100,000 + .8 x S)**
Since profit, or P, is 0 at the break-even point: **0 = S – ($100,000 + .8S), or**
                                                    S = $100,000 + .8S

Solving for S: S – .8S = $100,000
                                                    .2S = $100,000
                                                    S = $500,000

This means you would have to chalk up $500,000 in sales just to cover your total costs.

Profit From Your Budget

4

Few people enjoy budgeting. It takes time and requires self-restraint to stick to it. Nonetheless, there's no better way to keep a company on financial track than through a properly maintained budget program. Despite the almost universal distaste for budgetary restraints within departments, rarely is there a company today that operates without a budget. The key to successful budgeting is to involve managers in all departments and at all levels from the beginning stages.

The Budgeting Process

The budgeting process is an attempt to establish a set of realistic standards for the operation of a company. In its final form, the budget will be a set of specific objectives for the year ahead. Although these objectives are identified only after careful study, they are merely forecasts. Recognize that the original budget will probably need some revision.

The process only begins with the formulation of the budget itself. Every budgeting system must contain provisions not only for actually preparing the budget, but also for implementing a system, including coordination, control, follow-up and maintenance.

To be effective, a budget must be tailored to the specific needs of your company. Most well-designed budget programs share a number of characteristics, outlined as follows:

- **Clear lines of responsibility.** To succeed, your budgeting team must be able to assign definite responsibility for the performance of each unit measured. The person assigned this responsibility must have full authority to apply the standards set down in the budget.
- **Management support.** An unsupported budget will almost surely fail. Your operating departments must know that you will use the budget as a tool for measuring their performance.
- **Clear-cut reporting procedures.** When finished, your budget should be a projection of what your financial standards will look like at some point in the future. Therefore, the more closely your budget system follows your accounting and reporting classification, the better its chances for success.
- **Realistic standards.** Don't expect your budget program to work miracles overnight. The most effective ones set the stage for achievable income and cost improvements during the year. They are designed to foster continuous improvement in operating performance. The budget is just one of many tools in this ongoing effort, but one that is effective in pointing out the weak spots.

Developing a Budget System That's Right for You

There are three basic approaches to budgeting, each with innumerable variations. In this section we examine the strengths and weaknesses of each approach.

1. **Budgeting from the top down:** In a small electronics components manufacturer, top management will generate the primary budget. Then the allocations are sent down to the various department managers for their estimates of expenses and profits.

- **Strengths:** This is by far the simplest approach to budgeting. It also ensures that management's goals are always reflected.

- **Weaknesses:** This type of budgeting assumes that management has the operational knowledge necessary to budget for every part of the organization. Also, the lack of participation by operating personnel can lead to a lack of support for, and commitment to, the budget.

➤ **Recommendation:** This approach is best suited to the smaller organization, where there is an easy familiarity between staff and line functions. In a smaller company, management is more likely to be aware of operational problems and can easily bring department heads into the discussions.

2. **Budgeting from the bottom up:** Budgeting begins at the operating level for a diversified, midsize plastics manufacturer. It gradually progresses up through higher management levels until it reaches the top echelons. At every level, personnel will review and revise it, but only within the confines of broad corporate objectives that are set down at the outset.

- **Strengths:** This type of budget provides every operating level with a greater understanding of the business. It also ensures active participation and greater commitment from lower management levels. Every manager knows what is expected in terms of performance during a specific budgetary period.
- **Weaknesses:** It requires a lot of time to move through the process and complete the necessary administrative procedures. Operating units will often tend to be very conservative in projecting revenues and overly liberal in allocating costs. Some may even hold back on performance to protect themselves.

➤ **Recommendation:** This budget system is best suited to a multiproduct company, where many diverse operations have to be included in a single budget. It requires a large staff, so the approach might not be effective in a small company.

3. **The two-pronged approach:** A high-tech company based in New England uses a combination of the two methods discussed above. Specific objectives for financial performance are established at the corporate level, and then are submitted to operating managers, who prepare budgets based on operating-level objectives. Their budgets are then approved, disapproved or revised by management and sent back down for possible further action by the departments. The process continues until a final budget is approved.

- **Strengths:** The formal budget represents a true meeting of the minds by all parties and requires participation at all management levels. Theoretically, this results in a commitment to agreed-upon goals.
- **Weaknesses:** The process can be very time-consuming if top management and operating departments can't agree on the basic objectives. It's also by far the most complicated approach. Schedules and surveys are usually necessary to support deliberations at virtually all management levels.

➤ **Recommendation:** This approach is best suited to a company that has developed a certain amount of sophistication in preparing budgets. The size of the company should not be an overwhelming consideration, but keep in mind that preparing the data necessary to back up this type of program will consume a significant number of person-hours.

Organizing a Budget Team

Once your company decides on a budgeting system, you can begin to assemble a team to oversee the process. Note that we have not included a permanent budget staff in our description of organization *(see next page)*, but prefer to use the talents of management personnel already in place in various departments. If you decide later that the company needs a permanent budget staff, you could add one under the aegis of the budget director.

The Budget Committee

The budget committee at one service company includes the president, chief operating officer and senior management from each division. Their principal tasks are to appoint a budget chairman and to oversee the entire budgeting process. Specific functions include:

- Resolving budgeting conflicts that might arise between departments or between the budget chairman and operating departments.
- Reviewing budget estimates and recommending changes, if necessary, to appropriate department or division heads.
- Reviewing performance reports and recommending action when needed.
- Approving the budget manual, which details the administrative procedures to be followed in compiling the budget and contains the forms and instructions necessary to compile the data.

The Budget Chairman

The budget chairman is responsible for coordinating the budget estimates developed by the line departments. He provides technical assistance to the operating departments, whenever necessary. Other functions include:

- Advising on budgetary matters to both the budget committee and those who are responsible for operations.
- Recommending procedures to be followed by those responsible for each budget component.
- Developing timetables for each stage of the budget.
- Compiling forms, schedules or tables necessary to complete the budget.
- Supplying support data, such as revenue or cost analysis, which could assist operating units.
- Recommending action to management based on budget results.
- Analyzing and interpreting variances between budgeted performance levels and actual results.

Team Budgeting

As business has grown steadily more complex, **team budgeting** has proven to be a valuable tool for drawing the management group together and directing its efforts toward common objectives. Using the team approach, each manager is called on to plan and budget—and will be judged on his performance—in his area of responsibility. To participate in this process, each manager is given accounting data about past and current operations.

What are the benefits of the team approach? Managers are encouraged to think ahead and be prepared for changing conditions. When they anticipate difficulties or problems, they can more easily avoid or correct them. The skills of the entire organization can be brought to bear in determining the most profitable courses of action. Through team budgeting, performance generally improves because the people responsible for attaining company objectives share in setting them. Finally, the conversion of each manager's plans into dollar-and-cents budgets provides her with a financial blueprint of her operations for the period ahead. This serves as a benchmark against which to measure a manager's performance and to spot trouble early.

A limitation of the team approach: Inadequate or faulty planning is the No. 1 reason why budgets fail. It's not unusual, for example, to have the budget (1) provide for a cost reduction, with no mention of who's going to accomplish it or how; or (2) project a sharp boost in sales, with no program spelling out how this will be done or at what cost. Opening up a budget process to key managers can increase the possibility of this kind of wishful thinking. It will be up to the top executive, during his or her review of the back-up budgets, to test the soundness of underlying plans.

A Look at Zero-Base Budgeting

Another currently popular approach to budgeting is zero-base budgeting. When President Carter decided in 1977 that the government would adopt zero-base budgeting, the concept mushroomed overnight from a subject principally of concern to financial executives and organizational heads into a matter of interest to all managers.

The name **zero-base budgeting (ZBB)** for businesses is misleading. Many people, recalling the government initiative, believe that ZBB is a tool for finding and eliminating unnecessary functions. That's not the case.

The fact is, in any organization most, if not all, of the functions currently performed are necessary to its continued operation. ZBB is usually applied to help management decide whether each of these functions will make its maximum contribution to the overall effectiveness of the organization at its present level of expenditure, a lower one or a higher one. In the process, some functions *may* be eliminated, but that happens under any kind of budgetary review. In many instances, ZBB results in the approval of sizable increases in funding for activities where the anticipated payoff warrants it.

ZBB is designed to help management relate expenditures to the results expected to be achieved. Each manager presents separate budget proposals for each function of the unit he manages. Thus, it is similar to the team budgeting approach. The separate proposals, called decision packages, are what differentiate ZBB from team budgeting or the more traditional type of budgeting process.

Example: Under conventional line-item budgeting, a personnel manager would specify departmental expenditures for salaries, supplies, payments to employment agencies, etc. Top management would then review the total of these costs. Under ZBB, the personnel manager would present separate sets of decision packages for each of the department's functional activities, such as recruiting and hiring, EEO compliance and benefits administration.

If your company decides to introduce ZBB and you, as a manager, are included in the process, you will receive instructions and forms from higher management. Although the odds are that no two organizations will go about it exactly the same way, the pattern in most organizations will follow these general steps:

1. **Identifying your objectives:** The secret of living successfully with ZBB lies in carefully and thoughtfully establishing objectives. Your best bet is to start from scratch by sitting down and making two lists: everything your unit must accomplish, as mandated by law or by higher management, and everything you would like to do or believe would improve the performance of your unit. This could include projects that have been shot down in the past. By all means, include your key subordinates in the thinking at this stage.
2. **Refining your objectives:** When you have completed your lists, you may end up with 20, 30 or more items. The next step is to consolidate them under more general categories. **Example:** A medical officer's lists might include yearly physicals for executives, employee health education, voluntary exercise classes, flu shots. All of these might fall into the category of preventive medicine.

If you wind up with six or fewer categories, you're ready to go on to the next step. (The number of decision packages a manager can propose is generally limited, as a practical matter, to five or six.) If you have more than six, you'll probably have to do some hard thinking about your priorities.

3. **Stating your objectives:** You are now ready to write up your objectives in final form for the decision packages. This is a critical step. You want to state, as clearly as possible, the purpose of your activity and the results you plan to achieve in relation to organizational goals. **Example:** Suppose you are the manager of security for a manufacturing plant. A good statement of objectives would be: "To protect—at the lowest possible cost—against losses due to pilferage, burglary, robbery, vandalism and fire, thus contributing to profit." By contrast, a poor statement would be: "To patrol the grounds with guards and dogs, and maintain the security of the fence and guard posts to prevent unauthorized activities." That is more a description of activity than a statement of goals.

4. **Supporting your objectives:** Once you have determined the objectives for each package, the next step is to explore alternative ways of reaching them. For established activities, the current method is always one alternative. Others might be to contract out the activity, eliminate it or combine it with another one.

Usually, managers are asked to specify two alternatives that have been considered, and explain briefly why they are not recommended. Sometimes this may seem like a meaningless exercise because the one best way is obvious to you. But the purpose is to ensure that you don't blind yourself to other possibilities, and this can often be helpful.

5. **Allocating costs:** After you've selected your preferred alternative for each objective, you have to decide how much should be spent to accomplish it. Your starting point will generally be your current budget and controllable-cost reports. One practical way to begin is to set up a worksheet showing line items down the left-hand side and objectives across the top. Then allocate your line items as best you can to each of the objectives. This shows your current level of effort (spending) and will be spelled out in a decision package.

Depending on the requirements established by your organization, you will also be expected to define two or more levels of effort in relation to each objective. If the current funding does not accomplish 100 percent of the objective you are recommending, then one or more of the additional levels will be higher than the present expenditure. You will also be asked to spell out some levels below the current funding that would be feasible, but not necessarily desirable. One of these may be a minimum level, below which it is not worthwhile to continue the function. Many organizations set figures in percentages for the lowest level of effort.

6. **Preparing your decision package:** Now you are ready to fill out the forms that will become your decision packages for each objective. Most organizations design their own, but each package should include the following:

- A description of goals or objectives for each level of effort (expenditure).
- A brief description of the activity to be undertaken and the costs involved.
- The expected benefit this level of effort will provide.
- The probable unfavorable consequences if the funding is not approved.

Usually, you will also be asked to note the alternatives that you considered but did not ultimately recommend.

Next, you must rank the completed packages in order of importance. If you have five objectives, you will have five sets of decision packages, each of which must be ranked against the others. Then the packages are sent on to your superior or to some other designated individual in the organization.

7. **Evaluating decision packages:** Evaluation procedures differ among organizations. Some businesses use a group system. Managers on a given level, working as a ranking committee, discuss one another's proposals and rank them before submitting them to the officer in charge of ZBB. In other cases, all decision packages go directly to top management.

Once management has decided which decision packages to accept and at which level of effort, the manager is usually notified by her immediate superior. The amounts approved then become the limits within which the manager prepares the conventional line-item budget. This is used, as usual, for accounting purposes and to monitor current expenditures during the year.

What Not to Expect From a Budget

There are limits to the benefits a budget has to offer—limits that management is sometimes slow to recognize. Here are some traps to avoid when implementing or reorganizing your own budget, whether it be for a department or a whole company:

✔ **No substitute for a cost-reduction program:** At one time management viewed its budget primarily as a cost-reduction tool. It provided meaningful reductions in costs during the first year or two after installation. After the fat had been trimmed, however, cost reductions became more difficult to achieve simply because there was a limit to the improvements an operating manager could produce without additional management support.

Once this limit had been approached, further tightening of budget standards was self-defeating. Operating managers, realizing that the new, more stringent budget standards could not be met, simply ignored them. Because management couldn't discharge all the managers, variances were overlooked and the budget became ineffective.

➤ **Observation:** Cost-reduction systems cost money. Whether it be new capital equipment, more sophisticated cost accounting, additional engineering support or a work-measurement program, a concerted program to reduce costs must involve much more than a budget. The budgeting function can help identify these needs and can spot the improvement when it comes. It cannot do the job alone, however.

✔ **Not written in stone:** All budgets should be subject to periodic review and revision. Budgets should never be regarded as the final word on how to run an operation. Yet, in many instances, operating managers attempt to adhere to outdated budgets, even though they recognize that the best interests of the company might be better served by a budget revision.

Example: A department head comes up with a good idea that will save money in the long run but will increase costs in the next few months. If you sidetrack the idea because of budgetary constraints, your company needs to revise its concept of budgeting. By the same token, an optimistic production plan not quickly altered in an economic downturn can play havoc with the company's finances.

✔ **No substitute for a long-range plan:** Many companies, after installing a formal budget, believe they have also taken care of any necessary planning. Nothing could be further from the truth. Corporate planning is akin to budgeting in many respects, but it is far afield in some all-important areas.

First, there is the **goal-setting function**. A budget usually assumes that the operations of the company will remain more or less intact for a time. A plan makes no such assumption. On the contrary, one of the purposes of planning is to set new goals for management. Second, there are **timing considerations**. By it's very nature, budgeting is concerned solely with short-range decisions. Budgets usually have a range of one year, broken down into quarters and months. By contrast, planning places primary emphasis on the long-term outlook. Five years is usually the minimum period involved in long-term planning.

➤ **Observation:** In truth, budgeting and planning complement each other. Companies that fail to take the time and effort to work out long-term goals often find that their short-term objectives are in conflict and are wasting corporate assets. Those who fail to set definite short-term plans may often find that long-range goals are unattainable simply because they were based on erroneous assumptions.

Should You Use a Fixed or Variable Budget?

5

Once you have determined your budgeting approach and have assigned certain functions to your staff, you can proceed to the next step: developing the budget itself. There are two formats you can use: fixed or variable. Each has its strengths and weaknesses. Your decision on which form to use will, in the final analysis, depend on what you want your budget to accomplish.

Fixed budgets are by far the most common, particularly in smaller companies. They are relatively simple to prepare but have definite limitations. Variable, or flexible, budgets require a bit more work to install. They are, however, much easier to adjust for inflation and for changes in the level of operating activity. The emergence of inflation as a relatively permanent fixture on the business scene—and its consequent impact on business activity—has inevitably led to the increased use of variable-budget techniques.

Limitations of a Fixed Budget

In a small metalworking firm using a fixed budget, preparations begin about midway through each fiscal year. Each department, with the help of accounting, prepares an operating-cost budget, which is then sent to senior management, who may revise it.

If revision is necessary, they will hold discussions and iron out their differences. Then, near the beginning of the new fiscal year, the new budget is circulated, complete with monthly activity goals and cost allowances for the entire year. Meanwhile, management has used the budget to establish overall sales and profit projections for the year, and has set capital expenditures as well.

➤ **Observation:** As long as sales or revenue stay reasonably close to budgeted levels, the earnings estimate and cost standards should hold up fairly well. However, should the activity level vary to any substantial degree from the original forecast, cost allowances will quickly get out of line.

How Rising Sales Can Affect a Fixed Budget

You are the manager of a production department for a midsize manufacturing company. The original budget called for your department to process 50,000 units in November. However, because business activity picked up, you actually processed 60,000 units. As a result of the extra volume, your direct labor costs for the month rose from a budgeted $10,000 to $11,000. Also, instead of consuming $1,500 in operating supplies during the month, your department used up $1,700 worth of supplies. As the month drew to a close, your budget report would look something like this:

	Budget	Actual	Variance
Production Units	50,000	60,000	10,000
Direct Labor	$10,000	$11,000	($1,000)
Operating Supplies	$ 1,500	$ 1,700	($ 200)

In other words, your department has handled a 20 percent increase in volume with only a 10 percent increase in two important expense areas—a commendable performance, by any standard. Yet the budget persists in assigning your department an unfavorable variance of $1,200. You are, in effect, being censured for your efficiency.

How Falling Sales Can Affect a Fixed Budget

Once again, assume that you are the manager of a department for a midsize manufacturer, with an activity budget of 50,000 units for the month and cost allowances of $10,000 and $1,500 for direct labor and operating supplies, respectively. This time, however, your actual volume slows to 40,000 units, which results in a $1,000 decline in direct labor costs and a $200 decline in the cost of operating supplies. Now your budget would be calculated like this:

	Budget	Actual	Variance
Production Units	50,000	40,000	(10,000)
Direct Labor	$10,000	$9,000	$1,000
Operating Supplies	$ 1,500	$1,300	$ 200

In this situation, your output has declined by 20 percent, but you have been able to slice costs by only 10 percent—not a very happy situation. Yet, by using a fixed-budget system, you are credited with a favorable variance of $1,200.

Comparing Changes

Obviously, good managers do not fall victim to illogical conclusions such as those described above. These examples do point out, however, the problem of attempting to control costs when using a fixed budget. Even if the cost-control manager recognizes a smaller rise in costs than volume increases would justify in your department, there is no attempt to measure your efficiency.

➤ **Observation:** A fixed budget provides no standards to use when you are measuring costs. As a result, an analyst winds up attempting to relate budgeted costs at budgeted levels of activity with actual costs at actual levels of activity. The relationship between the two is tenuous at best, and therefore it can sometimes lead to misinformation.

Using a Variable Budget

An integrated paper manufacturer with several plants uses a variable budget. It prepares prospective cost allowances for a range of activity levels, based on observed variable-cost relationships. Each plant's cost allowance is determined on the basis of the actual level of activity. Budget performance reports include both actual money spent and the budget allowance for each cost item, all at the actual activity level. Thus, management can compare budgeted costs with actual costs, both at actual levels of activity. Moreover, because costs are adjusted each month, profit projections can be brought up to date and refined, which allows management sufficient time to take any action necessary to keep operations at optimum levels.

The Need for Flexibility

Only a few firms are stable enough to allow for accurate monthly predictions of operating levels. Yearly forecasts may come close to actual sales, but an annual forecast is rarely sufficient to satisfy the manager who must plan day-to-day production schedules. To be effective, budgeting must be done in monthly increments. Because it is not possible to predict exactly what direction operations will take from month to month, the only logical answer is to build some flexibility into the budget program.

Budgeting After the Fact

The key to flexible budgeting is to establish budget allowances after the month ends. As soon as you know actual activity levels for the month, calculate allowances and send reports to department heads. Make every effort to send them out within a week to 10 days after the month ends.

Under a fixed budget, you can circulate the allowance for a given month well before the month begins. As a result, the delay involved in circulating budget reports for a variable system has understandably led to some confusion over its effectiveness. Some argue that if department heads are not informed of their budget allowances before the month begins, they cannot be held accountable for keeping within those allowances. While this argument unquestionably has merit, it is less imposing in practice than in theory.

Practically speaking, all good department heads are intimately familiar with the pace of activity in their department. They are aware of changes in the operating rate and can usually come up with a valid estimate of production for the full month after a week or so has elapsed. They may be surprised by sudden shifts in production, but management can avoid problems by keeping operating departments abreast of the latest production forecasts.

Getting What You Pay For

A variable budget will cost much more to implement than a fixed budget. Cost analysis is more detailed; the extra time and effort that go into it will take money. Once you have gathered the information, however, the cost of administering a variable budget will probably not differ too much from that of a fixed budget. Moreover, by using a flexible budget, you will set up more effective budget standards, resulting in tighter control over operating costs. Generally speaking, firms installing a variable budget find that, on balance, they save money under the new system.

Producing an Effective Budget, Step by Step

6

Whether you decide on a fixed or variable budget, or use a team or budget committee approach, there are general steps that any company takes on the way to getting out the budget document, as we will outline in this section.

Step 1: Develop a Sales Forecast

Once your budget organization is in place, the only remaining task of any consequence is to formulate a sales forecast. Those who intend to use a budget primarily as a cost-control device might question the need for a full-blown sales forecast. Nonetheless, a forecast of sales, broken down by months, can help maintain a smooth production schedule even if your company does not see the need for a concrete estimate of profits. It can also have a beneficial impact on inventory control and purchasing activities.

If you intend to use your sales forecast for profit estimates only, a general forecast will probably suffice. By contrast, if your company is considering a major capital expansion program, or intends to invest in long-term research and development, you may want to adopt a more sophisticated approach. The following is a rundown of several sales forecasting methods:

- **Sales force survey:** Ask each salesperson to estimate, by product and customers, the sales in his or her territory. Sometimes estimates from the field are augmented by supervisory projections, and the two are then reconciled.

  ➤ **Observation:** The primary benefits of this approach include obtaining the low-cost, active participation of the sales force and getting very detailed data. Drawbacks include possible unrealistic goals by the sales force, the inability to include forecasts for planned new products, and the fact that the forecast is not capable of pointing out any turning points in the market.

- **Product survey:** An industrial products company first identifies as many potential customers as possible. After the list is complete, prospects are polled on their buying plans for the year. Finally, results of the poll are used to compile an industry forecast. By applying the company's anticipated market share to each product, it can derive a forecast of sales.

  ➤ **Observation:** The product survey is helpful in broadening a company's list of customers and potential customers. In many instances, however, responses to the poll are not very thoughtful, particularly from prospects who have no relationship with the inquiring company. Moreover, the technique is expensive and usually inappropriate for a company that serves a large number of industries.

- **Consensus method:** The management of a consumer products manufacturer selects a number of experts, from both the company and outside sources, to provide sales forecasts along with their reasons for the forecasts. A coordinator summarizes the individual forecasts, circulates them and schedules a roundtable discussion about them. Sometimes, a second forecast is submitted.

  ➤ **Observation:** This method has several noteworthy drawbacks even though it solicits the help of outside sources and can be used to develop a consensus on new products as well as currently marketed items. It is entirely subjective because no quantitative data are used; it seldom contains details on product lines or geographic areas; and it can be extremely time-consuming.

- **Technical forecasts:** Many companies keep mounds of statistical data gleaned from raw sales reports. These reports are often used to supplement, or even substitute for, their annual sales forecasts. Two of the more frequently used technical tools are **trend projections** and **moving averages**.

With trend projections, past sales history is used to establish a trend line through the least-squares method, which today is carried out by computers. This trend line is then extrapolated and used as the basis for a sales forecast. In the case of moving averages, an average of sales for a specific period is compiled. Then, at predetermined intervals (usually each month), the oldest period is dropped, the newest added and a new moving average calculated. The monthly average is plotted on a chart to establish a trend.

- **Computer-based techniques:** The increased availability of computers for small and midsize companies has spawned a number of sophisticated forecasting techniques, formerly beyond the capability of smaller companies. Although these techniques still cost more than the methods mentioned earlier, they are now within the grasp of most companies.

Regression analysis involves a series of tests to determine which social and economic factors correlate with past sales. When an index or measurement that fits the sales pattern is found, it is used as the basis for projection. With **econometric models** a series of relevant regression factors are combined, and forecasts for them serve as a basis for the sales forecast.

Sales forecasts are extremely important in the budget process because all other activities are geared to the sales level. If the sales target is set too high, a surplus in capacity, personnel and inventories may result. If sales targets are set too low, sales and profits may be lost through stock-outs, delayed deliveries or inadequate customer service.

Step 2: Develop Measures of Activity

Before attempting to categorize costs, you need to work out a measure of activity for each operation. To translate the sales forecast (which uses units of product sold) into information that will be usable for the budget and department heads, find measures of activity (standard hours, tons, dozens, units, cubic yards, etc.) that are broadly applicable to your company and to each department.

Example: A manufacturing department could measure activity in terms of physical output (tons, pounds, bushels) or time (person-hours, actual production hours). A service company, such as a railroad or an airline, could use a numerical measurement (number of trips, passenger miles, ton miles).

Just make sure that the measurement can be used to identify similar costs in other departments, and that the measure is influenced primarily by volume. The most widely used measuring rod for costs is called **standard hours produced**. In this case, you multiply the time standard for a particular operation by the number of pieces produced. Usually the accountant or financial manager will handle the conversion of the unit sales forecast into dollars, based on guidelines previously established with respect to price.

If the budget is to be based on "no changes in price" or, say, a 5 percent price increase on all products for the entire period, it's a simple mathematical calculation. If, however, the guidelines called for varying price changes by products—different increases and decreases—and the changes are planned to take place during the period, the calculations will be slightly more complex. The financial manager will have to determine what percentage of the sales for the period are expected to take place prior to, and subsequent to, the price change for each product affected. A good starting point usually is past history.

Example: If a price increase is planned for April 1 (in an annual budget), and 25 percent of the business on a particular product is normally secured in the first quarter, the financial manager would convert 25 percent of the units at the old price and 75 percent at the new price. Before the conversion is made, however, the sales manager should check for any anticipated changes from past patterns.

Before computing gross margins—sales less product costs—the financial manager must be advised of the anticipated changes in product costs (materials, labor and factory overhead). Because these will be educated guesses, the changes are usually averaged and expressed as a percentage increase or decrease in current product costs. Some firms go a step further and estimate the changes by major elements—for example, materials up 5 percent, labor up 7 percent and factory overhead down 10 percent.

After gross margins are computed, the financial manager will have the first three entries for the preliminary profit-and-loss projection: sales, cost of goods sold and gross margin. He will also want to retain backup sheets showing how the figures were prepared. In some firms, the top executive may want to see the same items by product line for comparative purposes.

Step 3: Collect Historical Data

Collect information on what the company has spent in the past for all cost accounts, and determine to which department these costs have been allocated. Now is the time to make any changes in those allocations.

Realistic cost allocation is at the heart of any sound budget. With a variable budget, which requires these costs to be identified over a wide range of operating levels, the task is far more complicated and expensive than under a fixed budget. Budgeting, however, is not the only area in which management can use detailed cost data. Product pricing, long-range planning, marketing campaigns and many other corporate endeavors depend on proper identification of costs.

Step 4: Do Cost Analysis

Analyze each cost and categorize it as fixed, variable or mixed. Each category is discussed here.

- **Allocating fixed costs:** Essentially, fixed costs are a company's overhead. The term "fixed" does not imply that these costs never change, merely that they do not change as the firm's sales activity moves up and down.

Perhaps because of the use of the term "fixed," management is often inclined to accept fixed costs as a necessary part of business life. In fact, many fixed costs can, and should, be altered with changes in the product line or the purchase of capital equipment. For instance, a company may reduce the administrative staff after the addition of laborsaving devices, such as word processors. Insurance premiums are often adjusted downward after an insurance audit. Even depreciation, the most recognizable fixed cost, changes over time.

In other words, so-called fixed costs are not fixed at all. They can get out of hand just as variable costs often do. This is particularly true after a lengthy period of high activity. If your cost-analysis program does nothing more than point out this fact, it will be more than worth the effort.

Once you've properly identified fixed costs, however, the analysis is fairly straightforward. Essentially, two steps are involved: **investigation** and **allocation**. First, investigate the basic reason for incurring the cost, and what factors cause it to rise or fall. When you have identified these two ingredients, assign the cost to a product or products. As an example, you might allocate administrative costs among several product lines by using percentage of sales volume as a guide.

➤ **Caution:** Avoid the temptation to allocate fixed costs arbitrarily. In many companies, fixed costs are spread indiscriminately among all products. This results in one product being carried by another. It is this kind of corporate injustice that effective budgeting always seeks to uncover.

Second, after you have investigated a fixed cost and come to a decision as to how it is to be reallocated, be prepared to defend your decision. The reassignment of fixed costs can cause a furor in management circles. Production managers, for instance, will seldom sit by quietly while their departmental costs are raised. Similarly, marketing will be reluctant to see product costs raised to a point where they might require price changes. Keep in mind, however, that a budget is useful only if the information it uncovers is properly used.

- **Controlling variable costs:** A variable cost directly depends on the activity involved. As the activity rises and falls, the cost follows. If the activity ceases, no cost is incurred. Examples of variable or direct costs would include sales commissions, direct labor and raw materials costs.

Normally, pure variable costs represent an important part of the total costs of operating a company. Thus, they are also important to an effective budget, even though they are usually few in number. Because pure variable costs are so easily spotted and are directly related to a specific activity, there is rarely, if ever, a problem in proper allocation. From a budgeting standpoint, the primary problem in handling variable costs is the development of a workable control system.

➤ **Recommendation:** In most areas, a budget is, in and of itself, an effective device for controlling costs. With variable costs, however, a budget must be supplemented with labor and material standards to be truly effective. Usually, you can develop these standards from historical data if your company has not set production yardsticks. Past performance reports can be combined with cost information to generate reasonable budget standards. Use these standards to develop fair budget allowances.

- **Classifying mixed costs:** Relatively few costs can be described as purely variable or fixed. Most costs are composed of elements of both; some elements are fixed and others vary with the activity.

In some instances, companies assign mixed costs to either the fixed or variable category for simplicity. However, when a mixed cost is treated as purely variable, the budget will tend to be restrictive at lower levels of activity and loose at higher levels. If a mixed cost is regarded as fixed, the reverse is true: The budget will be loose at low production levels and tight at higher levels.

To resolve this allocation-of-cost problem, companies use scatter diagrams to estimate mixed costs. When a **linear** mixed cost is involved, for instance, a line drawn through the points will slope upward and to the right; this indicates that costs start at a fixed level, then rise with activity. When a **step** mixed cost is involved, the scatter diagram will indicate a sort of staircase pattern, involving a series of lines at higher and higher levels. In drawing the lines, the "eyeball" approach is the only practical one for the step costs. Use the least-squares method for linear costs.

Besides showing you mixed-cost relationships, scatter diagrams are used to demonstrate the impact of any cost. They are particularly useful in identifying an operating practice that needs improvement. Furthermore, the graphic presentation provided by the scatter diagram is helpful in bringing a point home to management.

Step 5: Determine Budget Allowances

For each cost, determine budget allowances, with a set amount budgeted for each fixed cost, and activity ranges established for variable and mixed costs. This entails setting up an overall expense budget for the company, as well as individual expense budgets for departments or sections of the company *(see page 36)*.

Expense Budget, Year Ending Dec. 31: ABC Corporation

	Full Year	1st Qtr.	2nd Qtr.	3rd Qtr.	4th Qtr.
Sales	$420,000	$90,000	$120,000	$80,000	$130,000
Less: **Fixed Costs**					
Sales					
Depreciation-Office	$ 1,200	$ 300	$ 300	$ 300	$ 300
Rent-Office	9,600	2,400	2,400	2,400	2,400
Administrative					
Salaries	$ 20,000	$ 5,000	$ 5,000	$ 5,000	$ 5,000
Insurance	2,200	550	550	550	550
Manufacturing					
Property Taxes	$ 2,600	$ 650	$ 650	$ 650	$ 650
Depreciation-Plant	3,000	750	750	750	750
Rent-Plant	5,000	1,250	1,250	1,250	1,250
Salary of Supt.	12,000	3,000	3,000	3,000	3,000
Total Fixed Costs	$ 55,600	$13,900	$13,900	$13,900	$13,900
Variable Costs					
Sales					
Commissions	$ 45,000	$ 8,850	$13,070	$ 9,125	$13,955
Administrative					
Supplies	$ 4,000	$ 820	$ 1,150	$ 795	$ 1,235
Bad Debt Expense	4,200	900	1,200	800	1,300
Manufacturing					
Direct Material	$ 63,000	$13,500	$18,000	$12,000	$19,500
Direct Labor	105,000	22,500	30,000	20,000	32,500
Total Variable Costs	$221,200	$46,570	$63,420	$42,720	$68,490
Mixed Costs					
Sales					
Advertising	$ 8,000	$ 1,500	$ 2,400	$ 1,500	$ 2,600
Telephone	4,000	850	1,100	800	1,250
Other Sales	12,000	2,500	3,200	2,500	3,800
Administrative					
Telephone	$ 2,000	$ 400	$ 550	$ 400	$ 650
Other Admin.	3,800	900	950	900	1,050
Manufacturing					
Heat & Power	$ 15,000	$ 3,000	$ 3,750	$ 3,500	$ 4,750
Factory Supplies	6,600	1,600	1,700	1,550	1,750
Total Mixed Costs	$ 51,400	$10,750	$13,650	$11,150	$15,850
Net Income From Operations	$ 91,800	$18,780	$29,030	$12,230	$31,760
Less: **Interest Expense**	600		300		300
Federal Income Taxes	41,952	8,639	13,216	5,626	14,471
Net Income	$ 49,248	$10,141	$15,514	$ 6,604	$16,989

All general expenses of the company must be covered. This is not a problem in most firms because the members of the budgeting team, as a group, are usually responsible for all expenses. If, for some reason, this is not the case—the top executive may believe that one or more individuals are not yet ready to participate in the budgeting process—the expenses of that function can be budgeted separately or included in the top executive's budget.

Before each manager prepares an expense budget, the company should provide certain guidelines:

- **What expenses should be budgeted?** In the past, it was common for companies preparing budgets to allocate the fixed expenses (rent, light, heat, power, etc.) to the various individual units on some basis, usually floor space occupied. More recently, the trend has been for each manager to budget only those expenses over which she has control. Fixed expenses are then carried in the general administrative budget of the top executive.
- **What will be the compensation policies?** These policies may change significantly along with the general economic climate (in a profit squeeze, for example), the condition of the labor market or the company's profit outlook. It is important, therefore, for individual managers to have guidelines with respect to the possibility of across-the-board cost-of-living increases or individual merit raises, overtime and, if applicable, raises for nonunion employees to adjust for union-negotiated wage hikes.
- **What will be the company's general policy on expenses?** If the company expects to have limitations on hiring, new projects or overall cost-cutting programs, it should communicate these to the department managers charged with submitting expense budgets. If the top executive thinks that one department's expenditures or one specific expense is currently out of line, he should also convey this point to the individuals involved.

Step 6: Review Expense Budgets

Unlike other steps in the budget process, the review of each expense budget generally takes place in a confidential meeting between the top executive or budget committee chairman and the responsible manager, rather than in a full meeting of the budgeting committee or group. It will be up to the top executive, however, to (1) make certain that any services or projects planned that impinge on other areas of the company are coordinated with the manager(s) involved, and (2) judge whether the level of activity planned properly supports the company's objectives.

Few top executives need any advice on how to probe recommended expenditures. There are, however, two situations that occur again and again in expense budgeting, and either one can substantially reduce the effectiveness of the budget process.

One dangerous situation arises when the budgets of all managers are not equally "tight." One manager may conscientiously budget a program difficult to achieve at the price, while the other gives himself plenty of leeway. This inequity soon becomes known and seriously affects performance. The second danger arises when the managers learn that no matter how tight the preliminary budget is, cuts will be made. Such an automatic budget-cutting policy is bound to boomerang because managers may merely pad their budgets to wind up with the amounts they really want.

Step 7: Estimate Profits

With cost allowances budgeted for each department, you can forecast monthly profits by subtracting costs from revenue anticipated in the sales forecast. The result will be preliminary profit or loss before federal taxes for the budget period.

To facilitate a review of the preliminary profit-and-loss budget, the financial manager should prepare certain comparative dollar figures and ratios. The specific comparisons chosen will vary among companies, but here are several that are often used:

- Profit in dollars and net profit as a percentage of sales for the budget compared with current and prior periods. (Profit dollars may be up but represent a smaller part of sales.)
- Budgeted expense figures compared with actual figures for the current and prior periods, showing percentage increases or decreases. It may be desirable to provide these comparisons both by departments (sales, financial, etc.) and by item of expense (total salaries, travel, telephone, etc.).
- Ratios of budgeted expenses to sales compared with ratios of actual expenses to sales, for current and prior periods. (Dollar expenses may be up but down in proportion to sales.) Again, it may be desirable to provide these ratios both for departments and individual products.
- The increase in the total number of employees contemplated by the budget. Control of the number of employees is often considered the key to any cost control because all costs are directly or indirectly related to people. The trends over a period of years shown by two ratios can be helpful in viewing the overall effectiveness of the organization: sales per employee and profit per employee. In both cases, the total number of employees is used.

Using Your Budget

Even moderate success in preparing the basic profit-and-loss budget will encourage the budget team or committee to branch out into other areas. The expense budget, illustrated in this section, then becomes a firm foundation on which to build a cash budget, used to estimate the flow of funds, and a capital spending budget, used to control the capital spending activities. Both of these topics will be covered in later sections.

Remember to Follow Up

The budgeting function only begins when a formal budget is installed and operating. The company needs to follow up to ensure that budgets are properly used and that steps are taken to improve efficiency of operations when the budget points out areas for possible improvement.

The heart of any sound budget follow-up system is the monthly **performance report**. Issued for all operating departments, this report details results of the manager's effort to keep within budget allocation. Data included in the reports vary from company to company, but almost all reports include budget allowances for the month; actual monthly spending; variance (difference between allowance and spending) for the month, whether favorable or unfavorable; and cumulative figures for the year on allowances, expenditures and variances.

Performance reports for a variable budget are not issued until the month is over. Consequently, it is important to send them to operating managers as soon as possible. Otherwise, department heads will regard the reports as obsolete and having little relationship to the problems of the day. No budget performance report should reach the operating department later than the 10th of the next month.

Revising Your Budget

Any budget is an unfinished document because circumstances change. Many times, the data on which a budget is based are incomplete—and even when they are sufficient, the human element can affect them. When the economy turns down, for example, an overly optimistic budget can quickly drain a company's financial resources and sometimes lead to a crisis before remedial steps are taken.

You can improve your company's performance significantly by moving from a static budget to a **rolling budget** system. A rolling budget is periodically adjusted to the forecast, on the basis of the latest developments, of what the scenario is likely to be in the future.

Most rolling budgets are made on a continuous 12-month basis, with adjustments made each quarter. For example, a rolling budget prepared in the second quarter of 2010 would run from July 1, 2010, to June 30, 2011. At the end of September, another adjustment would be made, and the new budget would cover the period beginning Oct. 1, 2010, and ending Sept. 30, 2011.

There are two distinct advantages to using a rolling budget: Your budget is a reflection of the most recent business data available, and it takes into account the latest input from your sales force and operating staff.

Managing Your Cash

7

Nothing is more indicative of the health of your company than cash flow. As the saying goes, "Profits are an opinion, but cash is a fact." All managers are aware that profits lend themselves to being "managed" during any one specific reporting period to achieve desired corporate or shareholder results. By contrast, your cash flow is an undeniable reality.

Cash management is an easy concept to envision if you think about your own personal checkbook. You have to ensure that enough money has been deposited in the bank to cover the checks you need to write. You count on being paid what is owed you so that you can pay your debts. The same is true of your company—the numbers are just bigger.

The real aim, then, of cash management is to ensure that the right amount of cash is available at all times to meet your company's needs and objectives. With an effective cash-management program, your company will neither be surprised by a developing cash shortage nor find itself stuck with excess cash that should be put to work.

A negative cash flow is not necessarily bad if it is planned as an opportunity cost directed toward yielding greater benefits in a foreseeable period. A cash surplus, by contrast, can cause your company almost as many problems as a deficit, even though they are less dire. A cash surplus represents assets that are making no contribution whatsoever to your firm. Even if these assets are invested wisely in financial investments, the yield in many instances will fall short of your company's return on investment. Unfortunately, there is little that can be done with short-term cash surpluses, except to seek out the best possible yields for them.

As a nonfinancial manager, your role in determining your company's cash flow may be minimal—but understanding it is vital. First, if you manage assets or have an effect on sales or overhead, you probably affect the company's cash flow. If so, you will likely face questions about either what you expect to bring in (sales forecasts) or what you expect to spend (capital expenditures or operating expenses). Your understanding of cash flow will enable you to answer these questions.

Plus, if you intend to ask for additional staff, resources or money for a proposed project, a look at your company's cash-flow analysis could give you ammunition. You might see that cash is tight in March, but a surplus is projected in September. Asking for money in February would not be as smart as asking for money in August.

Making Cash-Flow Decisions

To understand cash management, keep in mind these two basic principles: (1) Cash should not flow into and out of your firm indiscriminately; and (2) getting a handle on your cash-flow situation must involve not only a subtraction of payables from receivables, but a plan for dealing with the time lag between the two. Let's look at the major decisions you will have to make to adhere to these principles.

- **Timing changes:** The easiest way to raise or lower your cash flow is to change the tactical pattern in which cash normally flows into and out of your firm over relatively short periods of time—say, four to six months. You can speed up collections and/or delay cash outflows to ease a cash deficit.

Bear in mind, however, that changes in timing merely alter cash-flow patterns for limited periods without changing the amount. They should have no impact on the future performance of the firm, or on the firm's long-term investment, marketing and growth goals.

- **Policy changes:** Changes in policy for the sake of handling cash-flow imbalances have much longer-term effects than timing changes. Such changes involve a commitment to alter previously planned objectives in costs of operations; organization or replacement of plant and equipment; marketing and sales; and investment in new products or service development.

From an operational point of view, such policy decisions could include raising or lowering inventory levels, or an increase or decrease in research and development spending. From a financial standpoint, you could decide to change your policy on dividends or capital investment programs. Of the two, dividend policy is the more flexible.

Policy decisions that alter the future course of your business should not be made lightly. Although reversible, such decisions can prove very costly and therefore should be limited to those areas most susceptible to quick response.

- **Volume changes:** These changes are strictly operational in nature and always consist of cutbacks to reduce cash deficits. In addition to planned reductions in sales and/or production, you could reduce raw materials and work-in-process inventories.
- **Irreversible policy decisions:** In all likelihood, your most difficult cash-flow decisions will involve this area. By its very nature, this type of decision changes your firm in a fundamental way. Irreversible operational decisions, for example, almost always center on the disposal of assets. Conversely, you might seek to put surplus cash to use by acquiring a company or another product line.

Raising new capital is the most familiar financial method of handling a cash deficit. Equity financing is preferred under such circumstances because it does not add to your firm's obligations. It is not always possible, however, for a firm with a cash deficit to sell additional common or preferred stock. As a result, many companies are forced to raise new capital via the debt route, which means that future cash-flow management must take into account the need to meet debt obligations.

Using Your Cash Budget

Before you can come to grips with cash-management problems, you must first know how much cash will flow into and out of your company. Second, you should have an idea of when these cash inflows and outflows will take place. A properly prepared cash budget can help anticipate possible problems and even suggest solutions.

The cash budget is used primarily to spotlight periods of too little or too much cash rather than for continuous control. The former is usually the problem for smaller companies, and a cash budget can be invaluable. By pinpointing probable cash needs by period and amount, the company is afforded the time needed to obtain extra funds.

A cash budget is taken, in large measure, from an expense budget. It starts with a cash balance from the old year. Then, by using data obtained from the expense budget, it projects the actual ebb and flow of cash transactions for the period. For most businesses, cash inflows will come from three sources: sales, cash payments received on account and loans. Because some customers will purchase on account, the cash budget must reflect that payment will be made at a later date. This is an important factor: Accounts receivable, while vital, are not cash in hand and cannot be treated as such to run the business effectively.

Illustration: In condensed form, the expense and cash budgets for ABC Publishing Company appear on pages 42 and 43. Both budgets contain annual and quarterly estimates. Note that the cash budget indicates that ABC will need to borrow a total of $40,000 in the first quarter (primarily to pay income taxes) but will be able to pay it back, along with other borrowings, in the third quarter. Moreover, ABC should be able to pay a healthy $50,000 dividend in the fourth quarter and still carry over a reasonable cash balance into the coming year.

Expense Budget: ABC Publishing Company

	Full Yr.	1st Qtr.	2nd Qtr.	3rd Qtr.	4th Qtr.
Sales:	$600,000	$80,000	$300,000	$150,000	$70,000
Less: Fixed Costs					
Sales	$ 15,000	$ 3,750	$ 3,750	$ 3,750	$ 3,750
Administrative	28,000	7,000	7,000	7,000	7,000
Manufacturing	35,000	8,750	8,750	8,750	8,750
Total Fixed Costs	$ 78,000	$ 19,500	$ 19,500	$ 19,500	$ 19,500
Less: Variable Costs					
Sales	$ 55,000	$ 7,150	$ 27,500	$ 13,750	$ 6,600
Administrative	12,000	1,560	6,000	3,000	1,440
Manufacturing	230,000	29,900	115,000	57,500	27,600
Total Variable Costs	$ 297,000	$ 38,610	$ 148,500	$ 74,250	$ 35,640
Less: Mixed Costs					
Sales	$ 34,000	$ 4,300	$ 17,000	$ 8,500	$ 4,200
Administrative	8,000	1,000	4,000	2,000	1,000
Manufacturing	70,000	9,700	35,000	17,500	7,800
Total Mixed Costs	$ 112,000	$ 15,000	$ 56,000	$ 28,000	$ 13,000
Income From Operations	$ 113,000	$ 6,890	$ 76,000	$ 28,250	$ 1,860
Less: Interest Expense	2,000	—	1,000	—	1,000
Federal Inc. Taxes	$ 47,460	$ 6,170	$ 23,730	$ 11,865	$ 5,695
Net Income	$ 63,540	$ 720	$ 51,270	$ 16,385	($ 4,835)

➤ **Observation:** For purposes of illustration, we have used the same data for both the expense and cash budgets. In practice, the two are usually similar but can't be exactly alike because of the time lag between sales and collections. Moreover, estimates for operating expenses in a cash budget are usually somewhat more up to date than those used for an expense budget.

Where to Obtain the Right Cash-Flow Information

A cash budget can give you valuable information on your probable cash-flow trends over a 12-month period. However, to be effective in managing your liquid assets will require more than guesstimates. You'll need data on historical cash-flow patterns to judge whether your cash budget is realistic. And, if you are to take timely action to avert potential cash-flow problems, you must

Cash Budget: ABC Publishing Company

	Full Year	1st Qtr.	2nd Qtr.	3rd Qtr.	4th Qtr.
Beginning Cash Balance:	$ 16,000	$16,000	$ 11,430	$ 86,430	$ 63,880
Collections	600,000	80,000	300,000	150,000	70,000
Total Available Cash	$616,000	$96,000	$311,430	$236,430	$133,880
Less: **Cash Payments**					
Sales	$104,000	$15,200	$ 48,250	$ 26,000	$ 14,550
Administration	48,000	9,560	17,000	12,000	9,440
Manufacturing	335,000	48,350	158,750	83,750	44,150
Total Operating Expense	$487,000	$73,110	$224,000	$121,750	$ 68,140
Interest Expense	4,800	—	1,000	2,800	1,000
Federal Income Tax	47,460	47,460	—	—	—
Dividends	50,000	—	—	—	50,000
Bank Loan Payment	52,000	4,000	—	48,000	—
Cash Balance (Deficit)	(25,260)	(28,570)	86,430	63,880	14,740
Bank Borrowing	40,000	40,000	—	—	—
Ending Cash Balance	$ 14,740	$11,430	$ 86,430	$ 63,880	$ 14,740

have information on current cash movements. Finally, you will need to take a look at future cash flow to establish an appropriate policy.

Although cash flow is simple in concept, in practice it can be difficult to nail down. The primary problem is that no two firms have exactly the same cash-flow pattern. Firms have different critical factors that must be monitored and controlled. Therefore, every firm has different information needs, requiring that the information-gathering network be specifically tailored to its precise needs. This does not mean you must invent a methodology for gathering and analyzing cash-flow information. The methodology already exists. We will discuss two broad approaches that provide you with insights for your firm from two points of view.

Receipts and Disbursements Analysis

This is the oldest, most common method of measuring cash flow. Because it is based on information recorded in the receipts and disbursements log—a basic bookkeeping ledger common to virtually all firms—the information itself is easy to obtain and organize.

Most firms will come up with relatively few general headings for their receipts and payments. Those headings usually will fall into the following categories:

Receipts: There are only a limited number of ways for the average company to obtain cash. However, it is important to differentiate each of those in the receipt section of your analysis. Only if each category is properly identified can you properly monitor your cash receipts:

- **Collections.** These are funds received from your accounts receivable. Normally, this category will represent the bulk of your cash inflow.
- **Cash sales,** or sales not involving credit. These are usually the next largest category but stand far below collections in most companies.
- **Nonoperating income.** Many companies routinely take in income from sources not necessarily associated with their primary business. This type of income includes dividend or interest income from investments, rental or lease income, royalties, etc.
- **Special, nonrecurrent sources of income.** The most common items in this category are new financings (either investments or surplus fixed assets). However, you could include income from any unusual source in this category.

Disbursements: There are a number of payment categories that a firm can choose to identify in its analysis of cash flow. Here are some common headings that you might consider:

- **Supplier payments** usually head the list and can consist of cash payments as well as a reduction in accounts payable.
- **Wages and salaries** are difficult to control over the short term but can usually be managed over a period of time.
- **Overhead items,** such as heat, power, telephone and other utilities, property taxes or rent, are generally fixed and beyond management's control. Thus, you can usually bring these items together in one category.
- **Federal income taxes** can change rapidly and should be classified separately.
- **Recurrent payments,** such as interest on long-term bonds or dividend payments, should be grouped together under a separate heading.
- **Irregular or special financial obligations,** such as short-term loan repayments or special dividends, should also be classified in a separate category.
- **Capital expenditures** can sometimes be significant and, at other times, can amount to no more than a nominal influence on your cash payments. However, they should be classified separately whenever possible.
- **A special miscellaneous category** should be included for extraordinary items (such as the settlement of a lawsuit or a patent purchase) or any other significant, nonrecurring item.

Illustration: To carry on with our previous illustrations, we have compiled an analysis of receipts and disbursements for the ABC Publishing Company for the first quarter of the year by using data contained in the cash and expense budgets for that firm. Note that the figures for the actual cash flow are consistent, even though the classifications used have been rearranged to suit the format for a receipts and disbursements analysis.

We have confined our analysis to a single quarter, broken down into months. There is no need for you, however, to focus only on one quarter at a time. If the seasonal patterns for your company warrant, you might choose to consolidate the data semiannually, or even annually.

But to keep your analysis up to date, you will need to compile a new one each month. As the analysis on page 45 shows, there was a warning as early as January that cash flow would probably not be sufficient to cover income taxes payable at the end of March.

By the end of February, the evidence was conclusive. However, with the warning, ABC was able to negotiate a short-term loan that took care of the income tax payment and a modest debt repayment as well.

Receipts and Disbursements Analysis: ABC Publishing Company

	1st Qtr.	January	February	March
Receipts				
Collections	$ 62,000	$ 17,000	$ 25,000	$ 20,000
Cash Sales	18,000	4,000	5,000	9,000
Miscellaneous	—	—	—	—
Bank Loan	40,000	—	—	40,000
Total Receipts	**$ 120,000**	**$ 21,000**	**$ 30,000**	**$ 69,000**
Payments				
Suppliers	$ 16,610	$ 3,305	$ 5,105	$ 8,200
Wage & Salaries	34,500	10,500	11,000	13,000
Overhead	22,000	7,000	8,000	7,000
Taxes	47,460	—	—	47,460
Interest & Dividends	—	—	—	—
Debt Repayment	4,000	—	—	4,000
Special Items	—	—	—	—
Total Payments	**$ 124,570**	**$ 20,805**	**$ 24,105**	**$ 79,660**
Current Surplus (Deficit)	(4,570)	195	5,895	(10,660)
Cash Bal.— Beginning of Period	16,000	16,000	16,195	22,090
Cash Bal.—End of Period	**$ 11,430**	**$ 16,195**	**$ 22,090**	**$ 11,430**

Flow of Funds Analysis

Analyzing your cash flow by the flow-of-funds method is markedly different from using the receipts-and-disbursements method. In the latter method, information is organized by account, but information in a flow-of-funds analysis is organized along the lines of management responsibility. As a result, it will point to the management decision areas that will be involved in resolving any cash-flow problems that may occur.

Cash inflows: When viewed along the lines of management responsibility, cash can flow into your company in one of three ways. First, you can receive income from your operations. Next, you can receive income from a financing, whether it be bank loans, your credit lines or the sale of stock. Finally, you can convert a part of your assets into cash. This can be done by the actual sale of a fixed asset, such as land, a building or machinery, or by speeding up collection of accounts receivable or selling off inventories.

Cash outflows: As with cash inflow, cash can flow out of your firm in one of three ways when viewed along a management responsibility line. First, there are normally recurring payments, such as those for taxes, interest payments and dividends. Second, financing obligations may include a loan repayment, bond redemption or perhaps a reduction in your line of credit with suppliers. Finally, you may decide to increase your assets. You could do this by purchasing a fixed asset or by allowing current assets, such as accounts receivable or inventories, to rise.

Illustration: To turn once again to our previous example, you will find below a flow-of-funds analysis covering the first quarter of the year for ABC Publishing. For demonstration purposes, we have assumed that during the quarter, ABC reduced its inventories by $2,000, increased its accounts receivable by the same amount and bought a $10,000 book-binding machine on credit.

Flow of Funds Analysis: ABC Publishing Company

	1st Qtr.	January	February	March
Cash Inflows				
Income From Operations	$ 6,890	$ 195	$ 5,895	$ 800
Financing				
Bank Financing	40,000	—	—	40,000
New Supplier Credit	10,000	—	10,000	—
Disposal of Assets				
Fixed Assets	—	—	—	—
Current Assets	—	—	—	—
Inventories	2,000	2,000	—	—
Accounts Receivable	—	—	—	—
Total Cash Flow	**$ 58,890**	**$ 2,195**	**$ 15,895**	**$ 40,800**
Cash Outflows				
Recurring Payments				
Taxes	$ 47,460	—	—	47,460
Dividends	—	—	—	—
Interest	—	—	—	—
Financing				
Loan Repayment	4,000	—	—	4,000
Reduced Supplier Credit	—	—	—	—
Acquisition of Assets				
Fixed Assets	10,000	—	10,000	—
Current Assets	—	—	—	—
Inventories	—	—	—	—
Accounts Receivable	2,000	—	2,000	—
Total Cash Outflows	**$ 63,460**	**$ 0**	**$ 12,000**	**$ 51,460**
Current Surplus (Deficit)	**(4,570)**	**2,195**	**3,895**	**(10,660)**
Cash Bal.—Beginning of Period	16,000	16,000	18,195	22,090
Cash Bal.—End of Period	**$ 11,430**	**$ 18,195**	**$ 22,090**	**$ 11,430**

Once again, note how the end result jibes with both the receipts-and-disbursements analysis and the cash budget for ABC, even though the information provided by this analysis is entirely different. The cash flow is the same, no matter how it is presented, but there are a number of ways of looking at it.

Even a cursory glance at the flow-of-funds analysis will show that additional financing was necessary to pay the March tax bill. At the same time, a number of other points become apparent as well. First, the seasonal pattern of ABC's operation does not help the company. Even though cash outlays were kept to an absolute minimum in the first two months, the modest cash buildup was overwhelmed by out-of-pocket expenses in March. Moreover, even though the slack February period was the proper time to purchase new equipment, ABC would have been hard-pressed to come up with the extra cash if credit had not been available.

Also note that the flow-of-funds analysis does not give specifics on where the actual cash is being spent, just as the receipts-and-disbursements analysis makes no mention of management decision areas. Thus, while each method has blind spots, together they can provide you with the information you need to make timely decisions.

Forecasting Your Cash Flow

Either or both methods of cash-flow analysis will go a long way toward satisfying your cash-flow information needs. Because both are compiled on a monthly basis, you should be able to track current cash-flow patterns quite easily. In addition, the quarterly consolidations should provide the data necessary to determine whether the assumptions contained in your cash budget were realistic.

This leaves one important area to be addressed: the formidable task of forecasting cash flow. With cash flow being vital to the continued existence of your organization, it is essential that you attempt to predict future cash patterns, if only as a precaution against a possible severe cash squeeze somewhere down the road. However, there are other benefits as well.

Frequently, a cash-flow forecast will help you avoid a costly business mistake, or it will provide an early warning sign indicating the path to improved management control. It can also reveal the need to raise significant funds before a crisis, or it can point the way toward proper utilization of an impending surplus. Even with these advantages, cash-flow forecasts can cause problems unless they are viewed in the proper context. Here are some key points:

- **Completely accurate forecasts are impossible.** No matter how much time and attention you devote to your cash-flow forecast, it will probably be wide of the mark. Nevertheless, if properly prepared, a forecast can still yield valuable information by indicating what type of action you should take to avoid cash-flow problems.
- **Forecasts must establish timing.** Not only must you attempt to predict how much cash will flow into and out of your firm in the future, but also you must forecast when these flows will occur.
- **Multiple forecasts should be used.** Obviously, it would be difficult to develop a format that could make realistic forecasts of the extent and timing of cash flows from, say, one month to five years in the future. Indeed, even if such a forecast did exist, you might not find it all that useful. In a short-term forecast, you would probably want to emphasize the details of cash flows into and out of your company. The longer-term forecast would place the emphasis on the financial aspect of your strategic planning effort. For this reason, your cash-flow information needs will be best satisfied by dividing your forecast into separate areas, one directed at the short term and the other at identifying long-term trends.

Preparing a Short-Term Cash-Flow Forecast

Short-term cash-flow forecasts are designed to predict your company's cash flow for periods up to a year. In its final form, your forecast will look much like your receipts-and-disbursements analysis. As with that earlier exercise, the amount of detail you include in the forecasts is up to you and will largely depend on your industry and your own information requirements. Under most conditions, however, a relatively short list of headings, covering primarily those items that are subject to management control, will do.

The best way to prepare short-term cash forecasts is on a rolling monthly basis—that is, the first forecast of the year covers January to December; the next, February to the following January; the next, March through the following February and so on. In that way, you will receive the earliest possible warning of a cash emergency.

Role of Cash-Flow Assumptions

The first step in preparing your forecast is to take a close look at your cash-flow performance for the recent past. A review of the past several months can be most helpful in providing information on items such as inventory levels and accounts receivable.

Next, you must make several broad assumptions about your business for the next year. Is it likely to be a good year, a mediocre year or a bad one? Will costs rise at a faster rate than sales, or vice versa? Many times your assumptions will be wrong, and your forecast will suffer as a result. However, if you set your assumptions down and monitor them continually, you will know when they have fallen short of the mark. As a result, you will be prepared to change your forecast as events unfold.

Once you have made the necessary preparations, you can begin the actual forecasting procedure. As an illustration, refer back to the receipts-and-disbursements analysis for ABC Publishing. The line items on a short-term cash-flow forecast for this company would, in all likelihood, be unchanged from the receipts-and-disbursements analysis. The projection period would, however, extend for an entire year on a monthly basis, rather than over the three months shown in the analysis. Here, on a line-by-line basis, is how you make your short-term cash-flow projections:

- **Collections.** This is by far the most difficult item in the forecast and unquestionably one of the most critical. Keep in mind that your projections for the earliest one or two months of the forecast are likely to be the most accurate; you have your recent sales results and current accounts-receivable information already on hand.

After the first month or two, your cash budget and past collection experience will be your primary forecasting tools. Whatever the case, if you bring your forecast up to date on a monthly basis, you will always have time to refine your early estimates.

- **Cash sales.** Your sales forecast and past experience are your primary guides with this category. Although cash sales are not much easier to predict than collections, they are usually not as large and, therefore, not as critical to the forecast.
- **Miscellaneous receipts.** Recurring items, such as rents, interest and dividends, are simple matters of fact. Nonrecurring items, such as bank loans, are almost always known to management in advance.
- **Suppliers.** Next to collections, this item will probably require the most investigation. You will use primarily your sales forecast and inventory policy to determine supplier payments, but

will also factor in production scheduling, purchasing and your accounts-payable policy. Your forecasts for the first few months will be more reliable than those for the future.

- **Wages and salaries.** This item is usually predictable. The costs of overtime and part-time workers offer the most surprises.
- **Overhead.** Most of the items are payable on a regular basis, so there should be little difficulty in making a forecast for this category, provided that you remember to take price increases into consideration.
- **Financial obligations.** These include interest, dividends, taxes and debt repayment. Again, recurring items are known to management, and nonrecurring items are matters of management decision.
- **Special items.** This category is reserved for one-time decisions, such as the sale of an asset. All such matters involve a management decision and are therefore predictable.

Using a Long-Term Cash-Flow Forecast

There is a fundamental difference between long-term and short-term forecasts. Short-term forecasts are tactical and concerned with management control of an existing situation. Long-term forecasts are strategic and designed to assist in development of long-term financing plans that will meet management goals. As a result, forecasting your cash-flow needs for the long term is closely related to strategic planning. Just as it would be foolish to forecast future cash needs in the absence of specific goals, it would be fruitless to plan a course of action without providing enough cash to get there.

In general, your long-term cash forecast should mirror your company's planning horizon. Always keep in mind that the farther out the plan extends, the less reliable the forecast is likely to be. In our opinion, it is not possible to produce a detailed financial plan for a period longer than three years. Financial markets are too changeable to allow serious planning beyond that.

Adapt Flow-of-Funds Analysis

Just as the receipts-and-disbursements analysis provided a framework for a short-term cash forecast, the flow-of-funds analysis technique can be adapted to long-term forecasting. However, unlike the short-term forecast, some changes in the format used for the flow-of-funds analysis are necessary to separate the impact of operational and financial decisions.

Illustration: Take a look at the table on page 50, where we have used the information contained in the cash budget for ABC Publishing Company as the basis for a long-term cash forecast. We have also assumed that, as in the flow-of-funds analysis, ABC Publishing decreased inventories by $2,000 and raised accounts receivable by the same amount. In addition, the company purchased a binding machine for $10,000 on credit.

Obviously, this forecast is behind the times. In the real world, the forecast could have been made well before a cash budget was submitted and would extend out for three years or more. Nevertheless, it does demonstrate how closely a long-term forecast parallels a flow-of-funds analysis, while at the same time adding information that long-term planners would need to make intelligent decisions.

In ABC's case, no financial surprises are in store. Operating cash makes up more than half of the cash needed to meet obligations. The balance of the needed cash is easily met by a short-term loan and new credit.

Normally, long-term cash forecasts are updated annually as management reviews strategic plans and draws up new budgets. Therefore, even if the plan were a bit wide of the mark, ABC would have time to revise it in subsequent years. Remember that the first year of a long-term plan must always conform to forecasts made in the short-term plan. Otherwise, managers may find themselves at cross purposes with one another.

Following are the major categories of information in a long-term forecast:

- **Cash flow from operations.** This category is usually part of your strategic plan. As cash flow, this item is before interest, taxes and depreciation.

- **Taxes.** This is a fairly straightforward item, but don't overlook possible tax savings in the future.

- **Fixed assets (land, buildings, plant and equipment).** Payments due for the purchase of new assets are usually found in the company's capital budget. Don't forget the various costs associated with these assets, such as maintenance and routine administrative activities.

- **Noncash current assets.** These include inventories and accounts receivable. Inventory and credit policies do not change often, so you can usually apply past experience to sales projections for future years to obtain reasonable estimates for changes in inventory and/or accounts receivable.

- **Financial obligations (interest, dividends, repayment of loans or bonds).** It should be simple to forecast payments due on current obligations, but you may find it difficult to project interest and principal payments on future loans. Dividends are not mandatory, but for the sake of clarity, you should include them.

- **Net cash requirements.** If there is to be a cash surplus in your firm's future, you will first identify it here. Rather than a net cash requirement, you will come up with a net surplus. You can, of course, make plans to increase your dividends or to invest the surplus for a while.

- **Available cash.** This reflects drawings from both existing cash balances and cash equivalents (U.S. Treasury bills, certificates of deposit, etc.). A surplus to be invested would be treated as a negative item on this line.

Long-Term Cash Forecast: ABC Publishing Company

Cash Resources

Cash From Operations	$ 113,000
Less: Taxes	47,460
Internal Cash Flow	**$ 65,540**

Decrease (Increase) in Assets

Land & Buildings	—
Plant & Equipment	(10,000)
Inventories	2,000
Accounts Receivable	(2,000)
Net Asset Change	**(10,000)**

Net Operating Cash	**$ 55,540**

Financial Obligations

Interest	$ 4,800
Dividends	50,000
Loan Repayment	52,000
Total Obligations	**$ 106,800**

Net Cash Requirements	**$ 51,260**

Planned Financing

From Available Cash	$ 1,260
New Credit	10,000
New Borrowing:	
Short-Term	40,000
Long-Term	—
New Equity Capital	—
Total Financing	**$ 51,260**

- **New credit.** Planned purchases, such as the $10,000 binding machine cited in the illustration, are rather easy to identify. However, you may have to look closely to spot a possible need for additional extensions of credit with suppliers.
- **New sources of capital.** These final items are strictly the result of management decisions. They are the "balancing items" but also represent the end result of your firm's financial strategy.

Keeping Cash Flow Under Control

As you compile your cash forecasts, be they short or long term in nature, you are forced to come to grips with possible cash-flow problems. No sensible forecast would leave a potentially harmful cash-flow problem untouched. Your analyses of receipts and disbursements and of the flow of funds will allow you to make any necessary adjustments to bring the forecasts in line with reality.

The final information tool in the system is a monthly liquidity report, which is easily prepared from monthly statements and previous forecasts. It gives you the information necessary to make day-to-day working decisions concerning your cash flow.

Illustration: Preparing a liquidity report is more a matter of organizing your existing information rather than gathering new data. All the information needed for the report should be readily available shortly after the end of each month. For details on how your liquidity report might look, see the box below.

Liquidity Report

Balance—End of Month	Current Month Forecast	Current Month Actual	Percent Change	Forecast Coming Month
Cash on Hand and in Bank	_____	_____	_____	_____
Cash Equivalents				
(Short-Term Investments)	_____	_____	_____	_____
Accounts Receivable	_____	_____	_____	_____
Accounts Payable	_____	_____	_____	_____
Inventories	_____	_____	_____	_____
Unused Lines of Credit	_____	_____	_____	_____

The Cash-Flow Statement

Another way to keep your cash flow under control is to monitor it correctly. But be sure to use the right cash-flow yardsticks. Because it can be difficult to derive cash-flow information from the usual financial statements, many managers gauge their cash flow either by adding depreciation back into net income or by using working capital from operations as a substitute. Both measures, however, are often at odds with actual cash-flow performance and can give off confusing, or even misleading, signals.

- **Net income plus depreciation:** Even though many financial pros do use this formula (cash flow = net income + depreciation) to define cash flow, it's not entirely accurate. The formula represents more a measurement of profitability, or what some business researchers call gross cash flow, than net cash flow. For example, it's a paradox of business that companies with little or no growth usually have fewer cash problems than high-profit, rapid-growth firms.
- **Working capital from operations:** Again, some use the working capital formula (current assets – current liabilities = working capital) to measure cash flow. Even though working capital is expressed in dollars, it can't be spent like cash. Working capital is a concept that doesn't pay day-to-day bills; only cash does.

Flow-of-Funds Statement

A cash-basis presentation in your flow-of-funds statement avoids the potential problems of relying too heavily on working capital trends while, at the same time, quickly gives you a clear picture of your company's overall liquidity. The flow-of-funds or cash-flow statement can be structured a number of ways—none of them complicated—to reflect changes in your cash position.

To be useful, your flow-of-funds statement should tell you whether your operations are generating enough cash to support expenditures. Specifically, you will want to know how much cash was generated from operations, how much cash was used, and whether your net cash positions improved or deteriorated during the year. In condensed form, your statement might look like this:

ABC Corporation: Flow of Funds (000s)

Net cash provided by operations	$37,000
Uses of cash:	
Dividends	(20,000)
Interest (net of tax)	(5,000)
Financing activities	7,000
Increase (decrease) in net cash	$19,000
Net cash balance—	
beginning of year	$15,000
Net cash balance—end of year	$34,000

In this case, the net cash generated by ABC Corporation's overall operations was more than sufficient to take care of interest charges and a hefty dividend payment. Moreover, a financing provided a further increment to cash resources. All in all, cash and cash equivalents more than doubled during the year—an admirable performance.

➤ **Observation:** The definition of **net cash provided by operations** is the key to the statement. Normally, this figure encompasses cash raised from sales, less out-of-pocket costs of goods sold and other out-of-pocket expenses. **Cash sales** means just that. Notes and accounts receivable do not qualify and must be deducted from sales. However, if notes or accounts receivable decline, extra cash is coming into the company and sales should be adjusted upward. **Cash cost of goods sold** consists of the actual dollars spent for manufacturing during the period. An increase in inventory means that extra cash was spent, so the cost of goods sold should be adjusted upward. A downturn in inventories lowers your cost of goods sold. Conversely, a decrease in accounts or notes payable indicates additional cash payments and raises the cost of goods sold, while an increase lowers the item.

Keep in mind that you must also adjust other expenses to reflect cash transactions. If accrued liabilities declined, cash was used to pay them off, so add that amount to cash expenses. An increase in accrued liabilities should be deducted from cash expenses. If prepaid expenses rise, add the amount to cash expenses; if they decline, reduce cash expenses commensurately.

Making Your Cash Count

Be aware of the opportunities that can enhance the cash you have on hand to meet short-term expenses. For example: Participation in electronic funds transfer (EFT) programs generally leads to a reduction in payment costs, compared with the use of checks. Moreover, by arranging for discounts in return for fast payment, you can reduce receivable carrying costs.

Also consider keeping your money in money market accounts. By combining your present checking account with a money market deposit account, you can put your liquid assets to work and save yourself most activity fees in the bargain. Look for other ways or programs that banks have to improve cash management.

Managing a Financial Emergency

Even if you make all the right moves in managing your cash flow, including reliable forecasts, accurate analysis reports and up-to-date liquidity studies, you may still wind up in the midst of a financial emergency. The reason is simple: Many such emergencies are caused by events outside management's control, such as an international financial crisis or a severe recession.

All financial emergencies have one common characteristic: If not dealt with quickly, the resulting dilemmas create more problems and become a drag on every facet of operation and planning. For this reason, a financial contingency plan should be part and parcel of every cash-management program. The objective of your financial contingency plan should be to quicken your response time to unforeseen financial strains. No two financial contingency plans will be the same simply because no two companies are alike. Nevertheless, every plan should contain basic elements:

- **Develop an early warning system:** Earlier, we observed that early warning is the key to effective cash management. Nowhere is this more true than in dealing with a cash crisis.

The first step is to determine which key variables have the greatest impact on the financial viability of your firm. These variables will differ from firm to firm. For some, inventories will be the culprit. Still others might find loan interest to be the chief burden.

Also, keep close watch on the assumptions that have been built into your cash-flow forecasts. Oftentimes, the fact that one or more of the assumptions have proved invalid is the earliest warning sign of impending difficulty. For instance, if your forecast assumes that interest rates will drift lower and they go up instead, your company could be headed for trouble, particularly if you will need to do some financing.

Further, you should take a close look at your company's history to find the cause and cure of past financial crises. History may not repeat itself; but even if it doesn't, your knowledge of how past difficulties have been overcome should yield positive results when dealing with the next crisis.

- **Set your priorities:** Once you have identified an emerging financial crisis, you will need to know the following: (1) what can be done; (2) how long will it take; and (3) how much cash you can raise. The best way to obtain this information is to establish a list of priorities, organized around the four types of management decisions discussed in the beginning of this section. To that, you could add potential financing sources, so your priority list probably would wind up looking something like the sample on page 54.

Priority List

Type of Action	Estimated Cash	Response Time
Timing Changes		
Speed Collections	_____	_____
Delay Supplier Payments	_____	_____
Delay Capital Expenditure	_____	_____
Other	_____	_____
Policy Changes		
Reduce Inventory	_____	_____
Reduce Dividend	_____	_____
Cut Capital Expenditure	_____	_____
Reduce Expenses:		
Administration	_____	_____
Production	_____	_____
Sales	_____	_____
Volume Changes		
Cut Part-Time	_____	_____
Cut Overtime	_____	_____
Cut Shift	_____	_____
Layoffs	_____	_____
Irreversible Policy Changes		
Liquidate Assets	_____	_____
Financing:		
Short-Term	_____	_____
Long-Term	_____	_____
Equity	_____	_____

➤ **Observation:** Each type of action has its own strengths and drawbacks. For instance, timing changes are easy to implement but can go only so far and will merely delay the inevitable in a protracted crisis. Volume changes can change cash-flow patterns in a hurry but are effective only when the emergency is related to declining sales. Policy actions offer the most fertile field for cutting expenses, but they take time and can also delay a recovery. All things considered, the best approach usually involves a combination of decisions, each supplementing the other.

● **Establish an emergency reserve:** Once you understand what kind of actions can be taken in an emergency and how long they might take, you can set up a sort of insurance policy in the form of an emergency reserve.

The size of the reserve is up to you. It should depend, however, on the length of time it will take to mobilize your other cash resources, and the estimated size of a cash drain during an emergency. For example, if you estimate that it would take four business days for an initial emergency response to yield cash and your maximum cash drain could be as high as $5,000 per day in an emergency, you would need a reserve of $20,000 for full protection.

To be effective, the reserve must always be available at a moment's notice. Therefore, most traditional investments, such as Treasury bills, are out, even though they may be perfectly safe. Usually, such reserves are held in money market funds or in an interest-bearing account. However, an unused line of credit would suffice if the funds were committed by the bank.

Summary: The cash management system set forth in this section can make a considerable contribution to your firm. Thoughtfully used, it will identify cash-flow imbalances before they become major problems and point the way toward their solutions. Consequently, when your cash flow is on an even keel, you can devote much more time to another important matter: building your company's revenues in a scope and sequence that contribute directly and effectively to an overall profitable operation.

Capital Investment Basics

8

Now that you have a handle on budget and cash flow, it's time to move ahead with new projects. But first you must answer these questions: (1) Is there enough capital? (2) What projects will get priority?

The best time—indeed, the only proper time—to make capital investment decisions is well before the actual funds are needed. Far too often, capital spending plans are made on a crisis basis, with the "squeaky wheel getting the most grease." A slick presentation for someone's pet project is no true basis for committing part of the firm's financial resources, no matter how well intentioned that project may be. As a manager with decision-making authority, you need a long-term approach—a system that will enable you to analyze each proposal and then compare it with other possible projects.

How to Prepare a Capital Investment Proposal

Sooner or later, all serious capital spending proposals are submitted for inclusion in a capital budget. There they are classified, analyzed and evaluated before management makes a final decision on which proposals are most suited to the firm's needs and objectives. Keep in mind, however, that a successful capital investment program must take your company's long-range goals and objectives into account. Ideally, you and your staff should provide input in generating and developing capital spending proposals. You should always think in terms of contributing to overall business strategies when choosing among various spending proposals.

This link with strategic planning can be accomplished in a variety of ways, depending on your company's size and the complexity of its operations. Following is a brief rundown of the steps to take in preparing a capital spending proposal. They mirror many of the steps your firm uses in preparing a company-wide capital budget.

- **Establish objectives:** To set your department on the right growth plan, you must first decide where you want it to go. You must set long-term objectives and take into account top management's expectations for the future.
- **Develop strategies:** Once broad objectives have been established, your department can start to consider various strategies that would help your company achieve its long-term objectives.
- **Present proposals:** Make each proposal as detailed as possible and include estimated costs and preliminary projections of possible savings.

All these steps are essential because your plans will be competing with those of other units in the company. Upper management will evaluate and compare each unit's spending plans. Those not fitting into strategic goals, or that do not have a good balance between financial stability and growth potential, will end up on the chopping block.

Classifying Capital Spending Projects

Most firms tend to treat all capital spending projects alike, an approach that can sometimes lead to serious errors in judgment. There are at least four broad categories of capital projects, each requiring a different planning approach and corporate strategy.

1. **Mandated expenditures:** These are expenditures required by law, such as OSHA safety regulations or EPA requirements. In addition, you can include spending projects to protect against product liability lawsuits or possible product recall.
2. **Maintenance expenditures:** Projects in this category include all those necessary to maintain production levels. Existing facilities or equipment often require repairs or replacement. Because your company's output will be affected if the expenditures are not made, you should give capital spending for maintenance a high priority.
3. **Cost-saving expenditures:** This category includes all projects designed to make current operations more efficient or productive. Cost-saving proposals usually involve a choice between the existing method and proposed expenditure, so they should always be supplemented by cash-flow projections.
4. **Growth expenditures:** This is at once the most important and the most elusive category of capital spending. It includes all expenditures designed to stimulate your company's growth, whether by introducing new products, entering new markets, purchasing equipment, adding facilities or making acquisitions.

Although capital expenditures made for growth can exert a profound long-term influence on a firm, it is usually possible to defer them without undue penalties. For this reason, you should put growth investments at the low end of your capital budget priority scale. Seek funding for mandated and maintenance projects first because they are necessary to keep the firm functioning. Next come cost-saving projects, primarily because they can have an instant impact on the bottom line. Only after spending plans for the first three categories are final should you turn your attention to growth projects.

Avoiding Common Pitfalls

No system for allocating capital resources is foolproof. You can, however, cut down on your chances of making a mistake by exploring the following alternatives when planning your capital investment proposal:

- **Look for something better.** Resist the tendency to assume that the proposals that bubble up from your subordinates are the best available. To strengthen your planning, solicit ideas from the widest possible range of departments.
- **Be ready to branch out.** Another common failing is the tendency to concentrate on the familiar when seeking fund allocations. Too often, innovative programs are equated with risky programs, and therefore disregarded. Always be ready to accept change if a sound business case can be made for it.
- **Look to the longer term.** In many firms, projects with a short payback period get the inside track. Management tends to think in terms of current-year results and overlooks projects that promise only long-term profit opportunities. However, the primary purpose of capital investment is to ensure the long-term profitability of your firm. Thus, while short-term profits are important, always leave room for projects that will pay off over the longer term—and be prepared to argue for them.
- **Follow up on your capital program.** Once a project has been approved, make an effort to ensure that it meets stated objectives. This will assist you in spotting problems early on and enhance the effectiveness of the program.

Calculating Your True Capital Costs

Before you can make an intelligent decision on a capital investment project, you will need to find out how much the project would cost. Then you must come up with a reasonable idea of the expected rate of return. Knowing these facts will tell you whether you're in a strong position to request an allocation of your firm's limited resources.

Assessing the Cost of Debt

Note that the interest rate on loans or bonds used in financing a project is affected by the nature of the firm's other commitments. If a firm has committed itself to several high-risk projects, it will usually be required to pay a relatively high interest rate on a new undertaking, whether or not this venture is risky in itself. Other factors affecting a firm's cost of debt include the company's debt/equity position and the economic outlook for its industry.

For these reasons, it is never safe to assume that the debt costs used to justify one project will be applicable to another. Each time you start to review a new project, take the time to find out your company's current cost of debt from your firm's finance department. Because interest expense is a deductible item, the cost of long-term debt should always be expressed as an after-tax figure. Apart from that, figuring your cost of debt is a fairly straightforward process. Merely use the rate of interest that your bank would charge for additional borrowing; apply your current tax rate to obtain the after-tax cost of your debt.

Example: If your company is taxed at 34 percent and your interest rate on a new loan would be 12 percent, your after-tax debt cost comes to 7.9 percent (12 percent x 66 percent = 7.9 percent).

What Are Equity Costs?

Company managers generally view equity capital as cost free. Theoretically, you do not have to pay the capital back, so it's free, particularly if your company does not intend to pay dividends that year.

From a stockholder's viewpoint, however, the outlook is different. Every dollar of earnings retained in the firm is a dollar denied to the stockholders. In a sense, it is a "hidden" cost for stockholders, almost akin to a new investment in the firm. The reason that stockholders maintain their investment is the promise of future dividends and/or capital appreciation (that is, an increase in share prices). Since both dividends and share price improvement depend on future earnings per share, it is the most important factor in determining your equity costs.

The easiest way to calculate your equity costs is to use the inverse of the widely used price/earnings ratio as a measure. If you have a firm idea of the value of your common stock, you can easily work out your own price/earnings ratio. If not, you can use the P/E multiple of a similar publicly traded company as a guide. Once you have obtained an appropriate price/earnings multiple for your firm, merely divide the numeral 1 by that multiple to find your capital cost.

Illustration: You expect your firm to earn $1.75 per share this year. Your company's common stock is currently selling for $20. Thus, your price/earnings multiple is 11.4 ($20 ÷ $1.75). In other words, you need $1 in earnings to raise $11.40 in capital, a cost rate of 8.8 percent (1 ÷ 11.4).

Alternatively, you find that similar publicly traded companies are selling at P/E multiples ranging from 7.5 to 8.5. Taking the median, you determine that, for each $1 of earnings, you can raise $8 in new equity capital. Thus, the equity cost rate becomes 12.5 percent (1 ÷ 8).

➤**Observation:** When discussing equity capital, almost everyone thinks strictly in terms of common stock. Technically, that's not true. Preferred stock is also equity capital but with a difference. It is permanent capital, but it bears a fixed dividend rate, much like a bond. If your company has preferred stock outstanding, you should by all means determine its cost. Since most straight preferred issues sell on a yield (or interest-rate) basis, the best way to calculate your cost is to find a publicly traded preferred issue similar to your own.

Illustration: If your company has a 5 percent preferred issue outstanding with a $100 par value, you might note that a similar issue, General Motors preferred, paying a $5 dividend, is selling at about $48, providing a yield of 10.4 percent. The yield becomes your capital cost because that is the rate you would have to pay to raise additional funds via the preferred-stock route.

Ways to Measure Your Expected Return

Once you have established the probable cost of your anticipated capital investment, you will need a meaningful measure of the productivity of that capital so that you can realistically decide on the project's worth. For many firms, the cost of capital becomes, in effect, the **hurdle rate**—the rate that any new project must earn to qualify for approval.

At the outset, you should recognize that all methods of calculating the anticipated return of a capital investment require a peek into the future. Thus, no matter how sophisticated they may be, they are certain to be faulty to some degree. Because of this, many companies seek to improve the odds in their favor by using more than one method of calculating the expected return. Then if the proposed project fails to measure up on more than one scale, management can discard it.

There are three commonly used methods of evaluating capital investment projects, each with its own strengths and weaknesses and a number of variations. There is no right or wrong method. The proper method for you is the one that best fits your needs.

The Payback Method

The payback method is the oldest, most common technique of evaluating capital expenditures. Today, however, it is almost always used in conjunction with one of the more sophisticated methods of capital investment evaluation.

This straightforward calculation is:

Original net investment ÷ Annual earnings after tax = Depreciation = Payback period

The calculation technique used in the payback method is a model of simplicity. The capital to be invested in the project, plus costs, is measured against probable cash flow from the investment. From this measurement, the amount of time needed to break even, or the **payback period**, is calculated.

Illustration: Let's say the ABC Company purchases a new machine for $70,000 that will require another $40,000 in installation and training costs. Thus, its total capital investment is $110,000. The company also expects this new machine to improve its cash flow at the rate of $25,000 per year. You would calculate the payback period as follows:

$$\frac{\text{Capital investment}}{\text{Additional cash flow per year}} = \frac{\$110,000}{\$25,000} = 4.4 \text{ years}$$

Unfortunately, it is a rare capital investment that throws off equal amounts of cash flow each year. Normally, the amounts will vary each year, as business conditions change. More likely, the cash flow from the investment described above will look like this:

	Year				
	1	2	3	4	5
Annual cash flow ($000)	$30	$20	$25	$25	$30
Cumulative cash flow ($000)	$30	$50	$75	$100	$130

Because the capital investment will have generated total cash flow of $100,000 after the fourth year, and $130,000 after the fifth, we know that the payback period lies somewhere between four and five years.

To find out exactly when, merely divide the amount not yet paid back at the end of the fourth year by the amount of cash flow projected for the fifth year. In this case, it is:

$$\frac{\text{Capital shortfall at end of Year 4}}{\text{Cash flow projected for Year 5}} = \frac{\$10,000}{\$30,000} = 0.3 \text{ years}$$

Thus, the total payback period for this particular investment becomes 4.3 years, somewhat shorter than the payback period for the project when equal cash flow is assumed.

There are good and valid reasons for the enduring popularity of the payback evaluation method, even though now it is usually used in conjunction with other forms of measurement. The most important reasons are:

- **Simplicity.** The payback method is easy to calculate and just as easy to understand.
- **Good risk indication.** The payback method gives you a sound assessment of your risk. The longer the payback period, the greater the risk.

There are definite disadvantages to the payback system, which, in some cases, outweigh the advantages. Here are a few:

- **No profit measurement.** The payback method measures the ability of the project to recoup your investment. It says nothing about profit. Thus, it is difficult to strike a comparison with other investments.
- **No rate of return.** Payback analysis takes you only to the date when your investment is returned. Thus, no true rate of return is ascertainable because a rate of return would consider total cash flow over the project's life.
- **No consideration of money's time value.** The payback method gives the same value to cash flow to be received, say, five years from now, as cash received today. In a period of high interest rates, this can be a serious drawback.

Over the years, a number of variations of the payback method have cropped up, primarily as a result of attempts to adapt the payback method to the need for more precise data. Although these variations can help, they seldom represent the whole answer.

The **discounted payback** method is an attempt to wed the payback method to the **discounted cash flow** concept (see below), which gives recognition to the **time value of money**. You apply a discount factor that will allow the discounted cash flow to reach zero, or close to it, over a somewhat longer period than would normally be used. This method is not fully satisfactory because it uses an arbitrary discount rate. Ideally, the discount rate should represent some sort of corporate objective, such as capital costs, rate of return and average industry return.

The **reciprocal payback** technique merely reverses the method of calculating the payback period in order to give an approximate return on investment rate. For instance, the approximate return on investment for our previous example would look like this:

$$\frac{\$25,000}{\$110,000} = 22.7\%$$

Keep in mind, however, that this is, at best, an approximation. Moreover, it should not be used if cash flows vary from year to year.

Using Net Present Value to Measure Return

If your company has not yet used the net present value (NPV) method of measuring the rate of return on a proposed capital investment project, chances are good that it will do so in the near future. During the past several years, NPV has become one of the most commonly used methods of capital investment evaluation.

For a number of reasons, the popularity of the NPV method has grown rapidly. Most important, it recognizes the impact that inflation or high interest rates are likely to have on the worth of a new capital investment. However, even with the cooling of inflation and an accompanying softness in interest rates, the NPV method is likely to retain most, if not all, of its popularity. Here are the reasons why:

- **Recognition of the time value of money.** Essentially, the concept of time value holds that a dollar received today is worth more than a dollar to be received later because (1) inflation erodes purchasing power, and (2) a dollar received today can be invested to earn interest.
- **Allowance of comparison of projects.** You can apply the NPV technique to all types of projects and thereby can compare and rank your various options.
- **Applicability for the life of an investment.** NPV can be used to evaluate an investment over its entire life.

Although these advantages give NPV a considerable edge over the payback method in some areas, don't make the mistake of thinking the NPV method will solve all your capital evaluation problems. NPV has some basic flaws that can, at times, lead to unjustified conclusions. First, it is difficult to forecast cash flow. NPV requires that cash flow from a proposed capital investment venture be projected for at least five years, and sometimes more. Obviously, such forecasts may be subject to serious error, particularly in a volatile business climate. Second, there is an assumption of steady reinvestment. The NPV method assumes that all cash flows from the project can be reinvested at a chosen interest rate. (This rate is called the **discount rate** and is usually equivalent to the company's cost of capital.) This may not always be possible. Finally, NPV does not measure the profitability of a particular project, only the cash flow. Actual profits in future years may turn out to bear little resemblance to cash-flow projections.

Even though the NPV method is not, in and of itself, a basis for judging the worth of capital spending proposals, it can be a useful tool in your decision-making process. As with the payback method, however, it usually works best when used in conjunction with other evaluation methods.

Understanding the Discounting Concept

Both NPV and the **internal rate of return (IRR)**, the next evaluation method we will discuss, depend on the concept of **discounted cash flow (DCF)**. DCF is based on a principle that most businesspeople instinctively understand, but nevertheless find difficult to convey. In simple terms, DCF recognizes that money has a certain time value. A dollar received today is worth more than a dollar to be received next year because the dollar received today can be invested to earn more money. Specifically, each $1 that you receive today is worth roughly $1.08 the following year simply because you can reinvest today's dollar to earn a risk-free 8 percent at present.

In other words, a dollar that you are scheduled to receive next year is actually worth only $0.92 in today's dollar. That's a discount of 8 percent to make up for the interest forgone. Similarly, a dollar to be received two years from now would be worth approximately $0.86, with the 8 percent discount compounded over the two-year period. Over a three-year period, your $1 would be worth only $0.79, given a three-year 8 percent discount.

In a nutshell, that's how the technique of discounted cash flow works. The projected cash flow from a particular project is discounted year by year. In theory, the final figure arrived at represents the money to be received in terms of current dollars.

Discounting to Find NPV

Once you've grasped the concept of discounted cash flow, it is a simple matter to calculate net present value. First, select an appropriate discount rate, one that represents the minimum rate of return that is acceptable for new capital investments. Usually, the average cost-of-capital rate is used as a hurdle rate, but you can substitute other rates. The discount rate should be in keeping with your company's long- and short-term objectives. After selecting a discount rate, apply it to the projected cash flows for the project. Finally, total the cash flows. If the results are positive, the project will theoretically yield a profit. If not, there is good reason to question whether you will be able to recoup your investment.

Illustration: Say the ABC Company is now considering a $50,000 capital investment in a new piece of equipment. After $10,000 in installation costs, the new equipment is expected to yield annual net cash flows as follows:

Year 1	$15,000
Year 2	$15,000
Year 3	$15,000
Year 4	$17,500
Year 5	$20,000

Because the ABC Company's average capital cost rate *(see page 58)* is 8.8 percent, it sets a discount or hurdle rate of 9 percent. Each payment is then discounted by using a present value factor table, such as the one on page 63. Here is how the NPV calculations would look:

Year	Net Cash Flow	Discount Factor at 9%	Present Value
0	($60,000)	—	($60,000)
1	15,000	.917	13,755
2	15,000	.842	12,630
3	15,000	.772	11,580
4	17,500	.708	12,390
5	20,000	.650	13,000
Total	**$22,500**	**NPV**	**$3,355**

As you can see, the $22,500 theoretical "profit" projected for the investment before discounting boils down to a more mundane $3,355 on an NPV basis. Nevertheless, ABC should consider the investment: The company would not only recoup the investment but also earn a profit in the bargain.

Table 1: Present Value Factors

No. of Years	Discount Rate															
	5%	6%	7%	8%	9%	10%	11%	12%	13%	14%	15%	16%	17%	18%	19%	20%
1	.952	.943	.935	.926	.917	.909	.901	.893	.885	.887	.870	.862	.855	.848	.840	.833
2	.907	.890	.873	.857	.842	.826	.812	.797	.783	.770	.756	.743	.731	.718	.706	.694
3	.864	.840	.816	.794	.772	.751	.731	.712	.693	.675	.658	.641	.624	.609	.593	.579
4	.823	.792	.763	.735	.708	.683	.659	.636	.613	.592	.572	.552	.534	.516	.499	.482
5	.784	.747	.713	.681	.650	.621	.593	.567	.543	.519	.497	.476	.456	.437	.419	.402
6	.746	.705	.666	.630	.596	.565	.535	.507	.480	.456	.432	.410	.390	.370	.352	.335
7	.711	.665	.663	.584	.547	.513	.419	.452	.425	.400	.376	.354	.333	.314	.296	.279
8	.677	.627	.582	.540	.502	.467	.434	.404	.376	.351	.327	.305	.285	.266	.249	.233
9	.645	.592	.544	.500	.460	.424	.391	.361	.333	.308	.284	.263	.243	.226	.209	.194
10	.614	.558	.508	.463	.422	.386	.352	.322	.295	.270	.247	.227	.208	.191	.176	.162
15	.481	.417	.362	.315	.275	.239	.209	.183	.160	.140	.123	.108	.095	.084	.074	.065
20	.377	.312	.258	.215	.178	.149	.124	.104	.087	.073	.061	.051	.043	.037	.031	.026

To illustrate, however, how even a moderate shift in the discount rate can affect NPV calculations, let's assume ABC decides that the cost of capital was climbing and that, from here on in, it would use a hurdle rate of 11 percent. Now the NPV calculations would look like this:

Year	Net Cash Flow	Discount Factor at 11%	Present Value
0	($60,000)	—	($60,000)
1	15,000	.901	13,515
2	15,000	.812	12,180
3	15,000	.731	10,965
4	17,500	.659	11,532
5	20,000	.593	11,860
Total	$22,500	NPV	$ 52

Now the $22,500 profit has been transformed into a minuscule gain of only $52 over the five-year span. The project, therefore, is only marginally acceptable. As you can see, your experience with the NPV evaluation method will heavily depend on the hurdle rate that you've chosen.

Using Internal Rate of Return

The **internal rate of return (IRR)** evaluation method is akin to net present value because it is also based on the discounted cash flow principle. When using NPV, however, you always assign a discount rate. In the IRR method, you derive a discount rate through trial-and-error calculation. The IRR method attempts to determine the internal rate of return of a proposed capital investment by calculating the discount rate needed to bring the NPV to zero. Then, if the calculated rate of return is greater than the average cost of capital, the project is acceptable. If not, the project is rejected.

By using a derived discount rate rather than an assigned rate, the IRR method eliminates one of the possible misuses of the NPV approach: arbitrarily using an unjustified hurdle rate. Nevertheless, the IRR method is still vulnerable to the basic flaws found in any evaluation system tied to discounted cash flow: namely, the wide margin for error in forecasting cash flows.

Even with these caveats in mind, however, the IRR can be a useful tool in measuring the rate of return of a capital investment project. Once developed, an internal rate of return can be compared to that for other projects and to your company's overall objectives, as well as the cost of capital.

Calculating Internal Rate of Return (IRR)

Year	Net Cash Flow	Discount Factor at 11%	Present Value at 11%	Discount Factor at 12%	Present Value at 12%
0	($60,000)	—	($60,000)	—	($60,000)
1	15,000	.901	13,515	.893	13,395
2	15,000	.812	12,180	.797	11,955
3	15,000	.731	10,965	.712	10,680
4	17,500	.659	11,532	.636	11,130
5	20,000	.593	11,860	.567	11,340
	$22,500		$ 52		($ 1,500)

IRR = 11% + ($52 ÷ $1,552) = 11.03%

Illustration: Assume that ABC Company is considering a $60,000 capital investment in new equipment. Expected cash flows are the same, but this time we will be using the IRR evaluation method. From prior NPV calculations, we know that the internal rate of return is somewhere between 11 percent, where a narrow profit was recorded, and 12 percent, which would certainly produce a loss. (*See box for the IRR calculation.*)

To find the exact rate, we interpolate. First, take the difference between the NPV at 11 percent and the NPV at 12 percent. In this case, the difference is $1,552. Next, divide the positive NPV of $52 by the $1,552 difference. Then add the quotient to the lower discount rate to get the internal rate of return, which equals 11.03 percent.

In the IRR method, the higher the internal rate of return, the better. Therefore, with an 11.03 percent rate of return and average capital costs of only 8.8 percent, the ABC Company would be well advised to give this project close consideration.

▶**Observation:** These are sound reasons for you to use all three capital spending evaluation methods described previously when preparing a capital budget. For instance, a payback analysis of the ABC Company project would disclose, at the outset, that this was a medium-risk project, with payback calculated in a little less than four years. In addition, the NPV analysis indicates that the new machinery will more than return its initial investment in the next five years. Finally, the project's IRR stands well above the company's hurdle rate. Because the project measures up favorably under all three evaluation scales, ABC Company management can be fairly confident that it will contribute to profits over the next several years.

In short, there is no need for you to pick and choose among the three evaluation techniques. Each is designed to give you a different insight, and you can profit from using all three. Equally important, by looking at the investment from three angles, you avoid placing too much emphasis on one narrow fact.

The Hurdle Point: Uses and Misuses

As we have pointed out, a hurdle rate is the minimum acceptable rate of return for a capital spending project. Originally, the average cost of capital rate was considered the hurdle rate because no firm can afford to earn less than its capital costs for long. Over time, however, the concept of hurdle rates has changed. All-inclusive, company-wide hurdle rates are giving way to a more flexible approach. Some hurdle rates are classified according to risk; others are assigned according to informal guidelines; still others are related to the company's strategic goals.

As a result, there are no hard-and-fast rules for setting a hurdle rate. It should depend on your company's objectives, the risk factor inherent in your business and the strength of your company's financial underpinnings. Nevertheless, you should keep some basic considerations in mind when deciding on a suitable hurdle rate for a proposed project.

1. **It should be based on reality.** This may sound obvious, but in far too many firms, the hurdle point is the result of an arbitrary management decision. In some cases, the hurdle point is too high and results in lost investment opportunities. In others, it is set too low, which usually leads to a strain on profits.

   Your hurdle rate should always be close to your average cost of capital. You should consider the overall trend of capital costs. If, for instance, inflation and rising interest rates are likely to push capital costs higher, you may want to compensate by raising your hurdle rate.

2. **It should bear some relationship to risk.** Your hurdle rate should be adjusted to compensate for the risks inherent in the project. The hurdle rate for low-risk projects need not be as high as the rate for projects with above-average risks. This includes internal risks, such as familiarity with the process, market or facility. More important, it includes external risks: the state of the economy, the outlook for interest rates, inflation, the business climate and so forth.

3. **It should be current.** No hurdle rate should ever be set in stone. As financial markets change, your cost of capital will change with them. Review your hurdle rate at least once a year, and in volatile times, consider revising it every six months. As a matter of fact, it is common practice among major companies to calculate average capital costs on an annual basis. The information is then usually passed along to the various operating divisions or departments, with each determining its own hurdle rate.

Determining Flexible Hurdle Rates

When properly used, flexible hurdle rates can provide reasonable yardsticks for judging prospective spending proposals, and they also avoid the pitfalls associated with using a single hurdle rate. To apply flexible hurdle rates to your capital spending program, you will need to rate each proposal according to its degree of risk. High-risk proposals should require a relatively high rate of return to be acceptable; medium-risk, a somewhat lower return; and low-risk proposals, an even lower rate. Minimum-return standards for each risk category are based on assumed-risk capital costs. This approach involves three basic, relatively easy steps:

- **Find appropriate debt/equity ratios** for each of the categories of risk. If you were to finance a high-risk project in the open market, you would probably have to do so largely by raising equity capital. These days, few banks are willing to take the chance of lending for risky enterprises. A medium-risk venture could probably be financed with a combination of new equity and a bank loan. In a low-risk venture, your banker would lend you most, if not all, of the needed funds.

While the precise debt/equity ratio used for each risk category will depend on your industry, the size of your company and your own financial underpinnings, there is a general pattern. The debt/equity ratio for most companies will fall within the following ranges:

High-risk: debt = 0%–20%   equity = 80%–100%
Medium-risk: debt = 30%–40%   equity = 60%–70%
Low-risk: debt = 80%–100%   equity = 0%–20%

- **Calculate after-tax debt and equity costs.** Next, establish a reasonable after-tax cost basis for raising new debt and equity capital. We can refer back to the example used in our discussion of capital costs *(see page 58)*. We will assume average debt costs of 7.9 percent and equity costs of 12.5 percent.
- **Calculate hurdle rates by computing a weighted cost of capital** for each category. First, determine what percentages of the total financing for a given project will be accounted for by debt and equity, based on the guidelines that were mentioned above. Then multiply each percentage by the appropriate cost of capital to get the **weighted cost of capital**. The sum of the weighted costs is your minimum return, a desirable rate for each risk classification.

Illustration: Using earlier examples, here is how to calculate typical hurdle rates:

High-risk (10% debt, 90% equity)
Debt	7.9% x .10	=	0.79
Equity	12.5% x .90	=	11.25
Capital cost		=	12.04%

Medium-risk (35% debt, 65% equity)
Debt	7.9% x .35	=	2.77
Equity	12.5% x .65	=	8.12
Capital cost		=	10.89%

Low-risk (90% debt, 10% equity)
Debt	7.9% x .90	=	7.11
Equity	12.5% x .10	=	1.25
Capital cost		=	8.36%

➤**Observation:** The crucial element in using flexible hurdle rates is your assessment of the risk involved in each project. How do you determine the difference between a medium-risk project and a high-risk one? This leads directly to the area of risk analysis, which we will discuss below.

Analyzing Your Capital Investment Risks

No capital investment project is ever without risk because there is no completely reliable way to forecast future cash flow. Nevertheless, there are various degrees of risk involved in different types of capital projects. For instance, the marketing of a new product, or entry into a new market, carries a higher risk than other types of projects. This is because management has no experience to draw on in this situation, which leads to imprecise cash-flow forecasts.

Thus, you can equate the risk in any given capital investment project with the probability of a variance in your projected cash flows. For instance, the replacement of a worn-out machine with a new one is usually a low-risk project. You have precise knowledge of (1) what the new machine can do, (2) how much more efficient it is than the old machine, and (3) the cost savings or productivity boosts that will result from replacement. Thus, the odds of a major deviation from cash-flow projections are small.

If you were given a choice between two projects with the same return, you almost certainly would choose the project with less risk. The higher-risk project could be justified only by a higher return. This is the why you must make some provision for assessing the risk in a proposed capital project. Without knowing the risk, you are not in a position to judge whether the project is suitable.

At the outset, you should recognize that risk analysis is a difficult job. No method of risk analysis is entirely satisfactory, and each requires a good deal of expertise and judgment on the part of management. Moreover, many risks are difficult to reduce to numbers. For this reason, you should regard the risk analysis methods discussed below as tools. They are not substitutes for sound business judgment. They do, however, force you to view the various projects in the same light, which highlights risk and permits you to compare all of them.

Weighted-Risk Analysis

In this type of analysis, you attempt to isolate those factors that would have the most impact on cash flow if they were altered. You can identify any number of key variables, such as a sales downturn, the time it takes to put the project into place, increased costs, an economic slowdown and marketing difficulties. After each key variable has been identified, it is changed slightly and NPV is recalculated on the basis of the different cash-flow assumptions. Then the effect of the change is noted and ranked.

Illustration: The ABC Company is considering introduction of a new product that has a net present value of $40,000 over five years. It determines that the most critical variables in its NPV calculations are anticipated sales, pre-production costs and distribution costs. The company then assumes a 10 percent change in each of these variables and recalculates NPV in all three cases. Assuming the following NPV figures, its weighted-risk analysis might look something like this:

	Change in Variable	Change in NPV
Sales	−10%	−30%
Distribution costs	+10%	−25%
Pre-production costs	+10%	−15%

In this case, a sales slowdown produces the greatest risk and trims the company's NPV by 30 percent, or $12,000 on a 10 percent sales dip. Also, it had better keep a watchful eye on distribution costs if the company does go ahead with the project. A 10 percent rise there will cut the NPV by $10,000. Pre-production costs are important but exert less impact than the first two variables.

➤ **Observation:** Weighted-risk analysis can be very informative, particularly if you are astute enough to isolate the key variables. However, this method also has some limitations. First, there is no provision for measuring the probability of changes in the key factors. Also, changes in a combination of less influential factors could result in a substantial change in cash flows.

Adjusting for Probabilities

Turn back once again to the ABC Company's illustration *(pages 62–64)*. We have already demonstrated that the project would be profitable at both 9 percent and 10 percent discount rates, but would produce only a marginal profit at 11 percent. Your company's finance department has likely developed estimates of the probability for each cost of capital, based on the outlook for your industry and economic projections. Obtain these estimates from the department.

A company estimates the probability of each discount rate for each year that the project will be in force. Then, NPV for each year is adjusted for the probability. **Example:** Refer to the table below. In Year 1, ABC estimates only a 10 percent chance of a 9 percent discount rate. Therefore, the 9 percent NPV of $13,755 becomes $1,375 ($13,755 x .10). Similarly, the 80 percent probability of a 10 percent discount rate translates into $13,635 x .80, or $10,908. Add to that the $1,351 from the 11 percent column ($13,515 x .10), and the adjusted NPV for Year 1 becomes $13,634. After adjusting for all five years, NPV is a positive $1,759 for the project—an indication that the ABC Company should proceed.

Probability Adjustment—ABC Company

| Year | Probability for | | | |
	Discount Rate of 9%	Discount Rate of 10%	Discount Rate of 11%	Adjusted Present Value
1	10%	80%	10%	$13,634
2	20	70	10	12,417
3	30	60	10	11,329
4	20	60	20	11,955
5	20	60	20	12,424
			Total Cash Flow	$61,759
			Capital Cost	60,000
			Adjusted NPV	$ 1,759

The attempt to measure the probability of different scenarios adds a new dimension to risk analysis and can be quite helpful. But remember that it is difficult to assign probability levels four or five years into the future.

Alternate Scenarios Measure Risk

With this method, you develop three separate NPV or IRR studies for each project. You assume that (1) everything will go exactly as planned, (2) nothing will go right, and (3) things will go more or less as expected, with some bugs. Then you compare the varying degree of risk in each project. For instance, you find two projects with the same midpoint NPV, but one with much more risk if nothing goes right. In that case, you would probably choose the project with the lower risk.

It is relatively easy to compare different projects with this method. However, it is also unrealistic in that there are few projects launched where everything goes right, and just as few where everything goes wrong. Moreover, there is no adjustment for the various probabilities.

How to Raise Money

9

Almost every healthy business will eventually reach a point when it must engage in capital formation. For some businesses, this time comes right at start-up, when funds are needed to pay the overhead costs associated with launching a business. Other firms look for sources of financing when they want to expand or move into new service areas.

All that you've learned in the previous pages is put to the true test when you're searching for capital. Not every investor is going to want to take a chance on your business. To make your search for capital a productive one, you must shop around for an investor whose goals and interests match your company's.

If you're a manager in a smaller company, there's a good chance you may find yourself sitting in the office of your local bank or a venture capitalist with your briefcase full of ratios, a balance sheet, forecasts, etc. Our aim here is to help you get the money you need.

If you're a nonfinancial manager in a midsize or large company, you're likely to be asked to participate in the fund-raising routine, especially if it involves one of your projects. You may not go to the bank with your CFO and ask for money, but you should be familiar with the process so that you know what's involved. Moreover, when you go before an internal board or committee to present plans for a new project, you need to take a professional, polished approach. Your plan should look like a business plan, with a description of the project, the competition and the expected payback. Use this section of our report as a checklist of factors to think about before you present your plan.

Keep a Business Plan on Hand

Unfortunately, many executives regard business plans as financing tools that are primarily useful for start-up companies or for those just emerging from the start-up phase. In truth, there are sound reasons for you to have an up-to-date business plan on hand at all times, no matter how successful or profitable your company. A solid business plan is an important financing tool at any stage of your company's development.

For example, your chances of raising equity capital without a business plan are virtually nil. No investment banker, venture capitalist or even a small business investment company (SBIC) *(see page 82)* would even consider a funding request without a formal business plan. Moreover, business plans are absolutely essential to the success of serious merger or acquisition negotiations. Even though banks and other lenders do not usually require a business plan (except for long-term loan applications), a well-structured plan can materially improve your chances of getting a loan.

Contents of a Business Plan

A typical business plan consists of three main sections, each containing specific information about your company's current business and financial position. The following is a brief summary of each element.

Introductory section: Usually only three to four pages, the first section is intended to give the reader a brief overview of the proposal. It should consist of the following: (1) a **title page** identifying the company and its principal officers, with names, addresses and phone numbers;

(2) a **table of contents,** listing the three principal sections and all major subheadings; and (3) a **brief statement of purpose** (approximately one-half page), summarizing the proposal, spelling out how much money is involved, how the funds are to be used, how the firm will benefit and how the funds will be repaid (in the case of a loan).

Descriptive section: The comments in this section should spell out your company's current business position and its plans for the future. Be certain to address at least these five areas by describing:

- **Your business.** As succinctly as possible, tell what your business is, how you run it and why you are successful.
- **Your market and your company's market niche.** Give some idea of your market's size and potential as well as your marketing strategy.
- **Your competition and how you handle it.** Mince no words. If competition is severe, say so.
- **Your management team.** Emphasize the business background and experience of each member. Include some personal data, such as age, special interests and place of residence.
- **How the new capital will be applied.** Spell out what projects the funds will be used for. You should be as specific as possible, which means that you will have to reach some hard decisions *before* seeking funds.

Financial section: Your "financials," as they are commonly tagged by lenders and other providers of capital, should be targeted at providing support for the statements made in the descriptive section. You will need both historical data and projections for the future. Start off with a Source and Application of Funding statement, which shows in detail how the proceeds of the financing will be used (for example, percentages allocated to equipment, advertising, product distribution). You can then move on to the more traditional financial statements:

- **Historical statements** should go back about five years in most cases. If your business is cyclical in nature, however, you should cover a complete cycle, even if it means digging further into the past. The reports should include balance sheets, income statements and cash-flow statements.
- **Projections** should also include pro-forma balance sheets, income statements and cash-flow statements. Summary reports are acceptable in most cases. Be sure to include projections for at least the period during which the funds will be used and repaid.

When a Shorter Proposal Will Do

Usually, you will need a full-blown 12-page business plan to ensure proper treatment on most financing expeditions. But there are times when a less thorough treatment will suffice. For instance, you may already have established a close relationship with your bank and merely need to present a documented proposal to the loan committee. Or, you may be attempting to arrange new financing from a private investor who is already familiar with your company's operation. In such cases, you can usually substitute a summary financing proposal for a formal business plan.

A summary financing proposal is a mini business plan consisting of no more than six or seven pages. The first page contains the proposal itself, detailing the amount of cash needed, repayment schedule, collateral and any other pertinent details. The second page summarizes how the funds will be used and how your firm will benefit. Briefly, this section sets forth your arguments on why the proposal would be a good loan or investment. This is followed by a two- to three-page outline on your company's history, its product and marketing position, the management team and a summary of its prospects for the future. In short, this is a capsule version of the descriptive section of a formal business plan.

Finally, you should include a condensed balance sheet and income statement, plus a year or two of projections. Cash-flow statements would give a substantial boost to your argument here.

Where to Look for Funds

Companies raise money for expansion in three ways. First, businesses can use retained earnings, which is the money they earn through their operations and do not distribute as dividends to shareholders. This simply means paying for an expansion project with the cash you generate through profits, similar to the everyday personal purchases you make. The second method is borrowing, and the third is equity financing (the selling of shares to investors).

Internal Financing

Your top source of capital is your company's own cash. It comes from sales and shows up in profits. Yet, although internal sources are obvious, many financial planners overlook them when they are devising capital formation schemes.

Many internal financing schemes boil down to cash management. Plus, attention to cash management early in the financial planning process has value even if you can't rely solely on internal sources. Effective cash management will help convince lenders and investors that you really know how to run a company and that you'll treat their money with the respect it deserves.

Capital formation begins with your company's cash budgets. As explained, the real aim of cash management is to ensure you have the amount of cash you need just when you need it. There's another advantage of careful cash management. Oftentimes, comparing actual cash flow with your predictions can signal an early warning of the need to improve management controls. You can avoid costly mistakes by taking steps to head off a flow in the wrong direction before it becomes a flood. Some keys to improving your cash management:

- Keep your money in money market accounts. Not only will you earn interest, but you'll be eligible for bank services, such as checking, at a reduced rate.
- Use electronic funds transfer instead of certified checks. Doing so will lower your bank costs and keep money working as long as possible.
- Offer discounts for customers who pay off their accounts early. This will reduce the costs you incur carrying receivables and will accelerate cash flow.

Carefully manage inventory, accounts receivable, accounts payable and surplus cash, and think of ways to increase sales. The next thing you know, you've got the capital to move to the next step in your growth plan. A penny-wise approach may give more obvious benefits to large companies with large amounts of pennies, but proportionally it will work for smaller companies as well.

Customers Come First

More companies are turning to their customers and vendors as potential sources of financing. New technologies have made so many businesses interdependent that the lines are often blurred as to where one company's function ends and the other begins. According to Rick Canada, director of change management services at Motorola: "The best definition of a partnership . . . is when the buyer and the seller take on the characteristics of one organization, rather than two separate, distinct organizations." When this occurs, it often forges a type of business marriage or partnership in which two or more companies share the costs, risks and profits of a particular venture.

Make Your Employees Owners

Employee stock ownership plans (ESOPs) are employee trust funds to which an employer contributes stock in the company at no cost to the employee. They are structured, however, so that tax advantages allow the company to borrow money at a nominal cost.

Until recently, ESOPs have been used primarily to shore up shaky companies. Usually, the troubled company turns over ownership rights (and risks) to employees in the hope of motivating the work force and securing "give-backs" on wages or benefits. Now, however, many successful companies are using ESOPs as funding vehicles because of their significant tax breaks.

Suppose, for instance, your firm wants to buy up part of its outstanding stock, but it doesn't have the necessary cash on hand. First, the company creates an ESOP. Next, it borrows the money to buy the shares and places those shares in the ESOP. To repay the loan, the firm makes cash contributions to the ESOP, and the ESOP pays the bank. In that way, both the principal and interest on the loan are fully tax deductible. As the loan is repaid, the ESOP stock is credited to accounts of employees participating in the plan.

ESOPs are not a one-shot deal. Year after year, a company can contribute what would normally be taxable profits to the ESOP, up to 25 percent of payroll. However, the contributions are made in stock—the company keeps the cash.

ESOPs can be valuable financing tools for midsize corporations, particularly closely held firms that might find it difficult to raise cash through normal channels.

The ABCs of Bank Borrowing

Asked why he robbed banks, Willy Sutton, a wily stick-up man, once said, "Because that's where the money is." If you're a small company, you probably do nearly all your financing through bank loans, which means that you'll be taking on debt. There are sound reasons for financing the growth of your company by using debt rather than the other principal form of financing—selling shares in the company.

Debt-service payments are a deductible business expense; dividend payments are not. When you issue new debt, you leverage your company to increase earnings potential. Issuing new common stock dilutes your earnings. Most important, new debt does not weaken control of the company, as would an equity financing.

If it's a bank you need, be sure to shop around and know what to look for. It's important, for instance, to find out which banks are in the best position to lend money—and may even be under pressure to make loans. In this respect, a key number to know is the bank's loan-to-deposit ratio. This will tell you what percentage of a bank's deposits is tied up in loans. Historically, the loan-to-deposit ratio was about 60 percent. Today, it's more like 73–75 percent. You can easily obtain this loan and deposit information through your state superintendent of banking.

Getting the most out of your banker: Even though banks supply well over 90 percent of the capital needs of small and midsize firms, few businesspeople take the trouble to develop a solid relationship with their bankers. It's true in both your personal finances and your business dealings: The best time to get to know your banker is when you don't need a loan. If you are in a position within your company to get to know the company's banker, take full advantage of that opportunity. It's a good idea to invite your banker on a tour of your facilities, and keep him informed of your company's progress by sending quarterly statements with appropriate comments to his office.

Even if you don't intend to borrow from your bank in the foreseeable future, a good banking relationship can help you in many other ways. For one thing, a banker makes an excellent character reference. As such, his endorsement might help in obtaining better terms from suppliers, equipment manufacturers and the like.

Presenting your case: By far, the most frequent mistake managers make in applying for a bank loan is to submit a late request for funds. To a banker, an emergency loan is anathema. It is an obvious sign of poor planning. No competent manager should ever allow a need that should have been anticipated to turn into a financial crisis. Thus, if you expect to have any chance of getting a bank loan approved, you must anticipate your cash needs well in advance, to provide enough time for the bank to process your application. It takes at least three weeks, and sometimes more, to process a loan.

Also make sure that you provide the proper information, which is similar to the ingredients found in your business plan. This includes the **financial statements** (going back three years is the norm, but some institutions prefer five years); **personal statements** describing the experience and capabilities of top management; and a **statement of purpose** detailing how the funds will be used, and how they will be repaid. A cash-flow budget covering the length of the loan is helpful, though not always required.

The loan interview: If you've done your homework, the battle will nearly be won by the time you appear for the loan interview. In many respects, your business plan or your supporting documents will do the talking for you. Nevertheless, you should take this interview seriously and be prepared to answer the banker's questions, which will be similar to these:

1. **How much?** Tell your banker exactly how much money you need. Don't be vague.
2. **How long?** Indicate how long the funds will be needed.
3. **What purpose?** Be specific about how you will use the money. "General corporate purpose" is no answer.
4. **How will you repay?** Again, be specific. If it's from cash flow, be prepared with a cash-flow projection for the duration of the loan.
5. **What if something goes wrong?** Prepare your ace in the hole: an emergency plan to use if the loan doesn't work out. You could plan to sell an asset, borrow elsewhere or have a new investor on tap. A sound emergency strategy can be most convincing.

Finding the Right Type of Loan

Despite the intimidating procedures involved in negotiating a loan, your banker *wants* to lend you money. That's the institution's business. He has to be certain, however, to keep the bank's money under control. One way to impress your banker is to speak his language; structure your loan proposal so that it fits neatly into one of the many loan categories that the bank uses. There is plenty of room for maneuvering within these categories, but to keep the bank comfortable, your loan request should fit into one of the following groups:

Short-term loans: Short-term credit is the backbone of commerce. Businesspeople use short-term loans (defined as loans maturing in one year or less) to finance everything from inventory to emergencies. Here are a few of the most common short-term loan classifications:

- **Time loans.** For companies with good credit ratings, the time or commercial loan is the chief source of financing. It keeps bookkeeping to a minimum and can be used for any purpose, including inventory and accounts receivable. Time loans usually mature in three to six months but can be refinanced for longer maturities.
- **Accounts receivable.** In this type of loan, the bank lends you 70–80 percent of the value of eligible receivables. As checks in payment for receivables come in, you forward them to the

bank, which deducts its portion and deposits the rest in your account. Interest is paid only on the amount of the loan outstanding. To be eligible for financing, receivables usually must be less than 60 days old, and your customers must be creditworthy.

- **Line of credit.** A line of credit is by far the simplest and most flexible short-term financing available for a business, especially a small one. There's a catch, though: Credit lines are usually granted only to the most creditworthy customers.

Medium-term loans: The principal difference between a short-term and medium-term loan is the importance of collateral. Medium-term loans are for up to five years and are normally used to finance equipment purchases or plant expansion. In granting such loans, the bank will usually expect you to pledge an asset that will generate the revenues needed to repay the loan.

A banker regards collateral as a safety valve. Although your ability to repay the loan out of your cash flow is the key factor in getting the loan approved, your bank will also request that the loan be supported by collateral, just in case something goes wrong. Here is a rundown on some of the most common asset types and how your bank is likely to regard them as collateral:

- **Liquid assets.** Money market accounts, savings deposits and bank certificates of deposit (CDs) can be taken at face value, as can short-term U.S. government securities such as Treasury bills. However, longer-term Treasury or municipal bonds are taken at market value. Listed stocks and bonds are usually discounted from market value, with the discount running as much as 25 percent.

- **Accounts receivable** can bring as much as 60–80 percent of face value, provided they are "eligible." This means weeding out older accounts, doubtful accounts and slow payers.

- **Inventories** are less valuable as collateral, primarily because they are more difficult to sell. Figure on an average of approximately 30 percent of the cost of raw materials and finished goods.

- **Machinery and equipment** are measured by auction value. You can usually use 50–70 percent of the auction value of machinery and equipment as collateral.

Term loans: Most term loans are written to cover the life of an asset or for a five-year period with a refinancing clause. They are written for 80–90 percent of an asset's total cost. Payments are made quarterly and consist of equal amounts of principal with interest computed on the outstanding loan balance.

Because small companies often find quarterly payments burdensome, many banks will work out a schedule of monthly payments. Most banks also will tailor payments to meet the company's needs, such as accepting lower payments in the early years of the loan and higher payments later.

Long-term loans: Long-term loans (over five years) have been virtually nonexistent for the past several years. From a businessperson's standpoint, the interest rate is too high, and the bank is hesitant to commit its capital for a long term when inflation might erode the value of the asset to be financed. When long-term loans are used, they almost always involve real property.

- **Business property mortgages.** In more stable times, commercial and industrial mortgages were not unlike residential mortgages. They ran for as long as 25 years and were paid off in monthly installments.

Nowadays, you may not be able to get a mortgage for more than five to 10 years. These mortgages usually involve equal monthly installments, with a balloon payment at the end. Only rarely is refinancing guaranteed, although most companies can negotiate a new deal when the balloon payment is due.

- **Real estate loans.** If you have substantial equity in your building, it may still be possible to arrange a second mortgage. Interest costs could be very high in some areas, however. A whole new refinancing package might also satisfy your cash needs, but you'll probably be swapping a low-cost mortgage for a higher one.

In short, unless you are certain that the return on your proposed new investment will be very high, you would be better off leaving the equity in your plant untapped.

The Loan Application

A lender will make you fill out a loan application. Typically, the application asks for a great deal of information, some of which will be contained in the business plan:

- The loan amount requested.
- How, when and from where it will be repaid.
- Description of collateral.
- Names, personal financial statements and income tax returns for anyone who will personally guarantee the loan.
- General information about the business: name, addresses, phone numbers, tax ID numbers, year-end statements.
- Type of business and history of the business.
- Structure, management and ownership, including résumés.
- List of other businesses that the owners control.

- Complete audited financial statements for the last three years, including balance sheets, income statements and projections through the end of the year.
- Cash-flow projections for the term of the note.
- Recent aging of accounts receivable.
- References from financial institutions with which your business has any kind of relationship.
- Customer references.
- Report on any significant developments for the business.
- Any additional material you want to include, such as brochures to help the lender understand the business.

Score Your Loan Worthiness

There's a limit to the amount of debt any company can handle. Thus, no matter how smooth your presentation, your bank (or any other lender) will always evaluate how much debt you can afford. If you want to gauge your chances of receiving a favorable reception at a bank, there are a couple of techniques you can use. Lenders traditionally look at two ratios to test your ability to repay:

1. **Interest coverage ratio:** earnings before interest and taxes divided by interest charges. This basic ratio defines your ability to meet interest payments on time. Inflation has led to altered standards for many ratios, but this one remains unchanged. You should have $3 of operating earnings for each $1 in interest charges.
2. **Debt-service ratio:** This ratio is calculated as follows:

$$\frac{\text{Earnings before interest and taxes}}{\text{Interest charges} + \dfrac{\text{Principal payments}}{1 - \text{tax rate}}}$$

Principal payments are adjusted for after-tax earnings because they are not tax deductible.

The interest coverage ratio says nothing about your ability to meet debt repayments. This ratio corrects that failing. A ratio of 1 is critical; anything less and your company is in danger of default. To be safe, a ratio of 2 or more is desirable.

In addition to these ratios, there's a technique called the **Zeta scoring system**. This is a proprietary computer model used by banks and other institutions to measure a company's vulnerability to financial difficulties. Even if your bank does not use the Zeta system itself, your Zeta score should give some indication of how you stand according to traditional financing benchmarks. The heart of the system is a group of financial ratios, each weighted according to its importance as an indicator of financial health. As with all numerical rating systems, the model has its flaws. Nevertheless, the Zeta scoring system has become one of the more common methods of evaluating a company's financial underpinnings.

You should encounter little difficulty in computing your company's Zeta score on your own by using data from your most recent financial statements. Here are the key elements and a hypothetical illustration of how they were used by the XYZ Mfg. Company:

- **Working capital.** First, divide working capital (current assets minus current liabilities) by total assets. Then, to obtain the proper weight, multiply by 1.2. XYZ's assets total $120 million, and working capital stands at $24 million. Thus, $24 million divided by $120 million = .20. When .20 is multiplied by 1.2, the Zeta factor is 0.24.
- **Cumulative profitability.** Here, you divide retained earnings by total assets. This measurement is weighted a little more heavily, so multiply the answer by 1.4. Retained earnings of XYZ amount to $54.4 million. The Zeta calculation for this component becomes $54.4 million divided by $120 million = 0.45 x 1.4 = 0.63.
- **Return on assets.** This measure of profitability is given the heaviest weight. Divide pretax profits by total assets. Then multiply your answer by 3.3. With pretax profits of $28.4 million, XYZ's Zeta calculation for return on assets becomes $28.4 million divided by $120 million = .24 x 3.3 = 0.79.
- **Return on sales.** Here, you measure how many sales dollars are generated by each dollar of assets. Divide sales by total assets. The weighting is neutral, so multiply by 1.0. Sales of $145 million for XYZ are divided by $120 million, producing a figure of 1.2. When multiplied by 1.0, the Zeta factor remains 1.2.
- **Leverage.** This final ratio is a bit different in that it attempts to measure the volatility of your company's capital structure. Divide shareholders' equity by your total debt. This final component is negatively weighted, so multiply by 0.6. XYZ's equity of $90.6 million is divided by a total debt of $33 million, producing a ratio of 2.75. This is multiplied by 0.6 for a Zeta factor of 1.65.

To arrive at your company's Zeta score, merely add the scores for each individual component. If your final score is 3.0 or more, you are in good financial shape, according to the Zeta system. A score of less than 2.0 indicates that some problems exist, and anything less than 1.8 places a firm in the high-risk category. A negative score is supposed to foreshadow imminent bankruptcy. In XYZ's case, the five components, added together, yield a total Zeta score of 4.51, or more than enough to justify a loan.

➤**Observation:** Zeta scores are seldom crucial to a banker's evaluation of your company. There are many other factors of at least equal importance. Nevertheless, if you find that your Zeta score is on the low side, you can prepare arguments to refute the implications. If you find that your Zeta score is satisfactory, you can cite it as evidence of financial health.

If Your Banker Turns You Down . . .

Most businesspeople have been turned down for a business loan at least once in their careers, and it can be a wrenching experience. If your loan request is refused, don't panic. Your company will probably prosper, even without the extra cash. However, you have some work to do.

The first task is to find out why you have been turned down. Ask your banker directly. Ask for specifics; don't settle for a vague answer, such as "undercapitalization." You can't correct the situation unless you know what is wrong. Most loan requests are turned down for one of the following reasons:

1. **Poor communication.** If you and the banker don't hit it off, the chances for your loan drop precipitously. *Solution:* Ask to be serviced by another loan officer. You have a right to expect that the person serving you will be empathetic about your problems.
2. **Uncontrolled expansion.** Banks shy away from a company with a revenue growth rate that surpasses its ability to finance necessary expansion. *Solution:* If you want to finance an expansion program, make certain that your business plan includes a full explanation of how your company expects to keep pace with sales growth.
3. **Overly optimistic business plan.** Your bank will check your sales and earnings forecasts against industrywide forecasts and may also match your projections against those of a company in a similar business. If your forecasts appear too optimistic, your loan will probably be turned down. *Solution:* Keep forecasts realistic, even conservative.
4. **Past misuse of loan funds.** If you use funds for a project not in your statement of purpose and the bank finds out, your chances of receiving another loan from that bank are slim. *Solution:* If circumstances beyond your control make it impossible to fulfill loan conditions, inform your bank at once.
5. **Rapid inventory buildup.** To a bank, a sudden surge in inventories means one of two things: poor planning or an unanticipated drop in sales. In either case, there is reason to hold off new credit. *Solution:* Make sure your inventories are in reasonable shape before you apply for a loan. Don't expect the bank to finance inventories above the range you normally carry.

No bank enjoys turning down a loan request. Apart from the fact that the bank makes money by lending funds, the bank understandably wants to be viewed favorably by its customers and prospective customers. Therefore, if you are turned down, you probably have the full sympathy of your banker at that moment. You might be able to use that sympathy as a bridge to your next move, by asking for your banker's help with such questions as: "What would you do if you were me?" or "What source should I try now?"

Loan Guarantees From the SBA

If you are turned down for a loan by your banker, you may apply for a loan guarantee by the Small Business Administration (SBA). Provided you meet certain risk requirements, the SBA can guarantee the loan. (In cities with a population of 200,000 or more, you must be turned down by two banks before applying for an SBA loan.) If you have a good relationship with your bank, it will process your loan through the SBA. This will require a great deal of documentation, including the usual business financial statements, plus the following: a **current personal financial statement** from all holders of 20 percent or more of the company's common stock; a **business plan** covering the period of the loan; and a **list of all collateral**, including the estimated market value of each item.

In the past, the attractiveness of SBA-guaranteed loans had dimmed because of the seemingly interminable amount of red tape and the time it took to get the loan approved. The SBA has become more innovative in attempting to reduce that lead time. In particular, a new program, dubbed the Preferred Lenders Program (PLP), can cut processing delays dramatically. PLP loans frequently can be processed in two to three days.

How PLP Works

One reason for this faster processing is that the Preferred Lenders Program turns over most of the paperwork to the bank lender. Whereas in prior years the principal responsibility for approval rested with the SBA, the PLP transfers that responsibility to the bank making the loan. Participating lenders can determine eligibility, creditworthiness and loan structuring, as well as make other decisions on their own, without prior review or consent by the SBA.

Under the Preferred Lenders Program, the amount of loan guaranteed by the SBA cannot exceed 75 percent. This compares with a guarantee rate of 90 percent on previous SBA programs.

If your area is not served by participating PLP lenders, keep in mind that the SBA still continues to operate its Certified Lenders Program (CLP). Under the CLP, participating lenders trained in handling SBA loan applications can obtain a decision and loan document package from the SBA within three working days. For more information about these and other programs, contact your local SBA office or visit www.sba.gov.

Loans From Commercial Finance Companies

If you have recently been turned down for a loan by a bank, you might receive a warmer welcome at a commercial finance company. Indeed, many banks, in rejecting a loan proposal, will refer a customer to a commercial finance subsidiary.

Commercial finance companies use a portion of a company's assets as collateral for business loans. Their lending standards are normally more liberal than those of banks. Rates, however, are generally higher and vary with the type of collateral and length of the loan. Generally, rates vary from 3 percent to 6 percent above prime on loans maturing in two to 15 years. The types of loans include:

- **Inventory loans.** In this type of loan, you use your inventory as collateral. The lender will advance funds at a certain percentage of your eligible inventories. There is no standard percentage, but because inventories are valued at distress or "knock-down" prices, the valuation is always conservative. You can count on from 25 percent to 50 percent of eligible inventories.

You supply a regular schedule of inventories to the lender, and the total amount of the loan is adjusted as inventories fluctuate. Generally, freely traded commodities receive the highest advances in an inventory loan, while difficult-to-sell, work-in-process inventories receive the lowest advances.

- **Equipment loans.** With these, you finance new equipment by borrowing against existing equipment. Machinery, rolling stock (vehicles) and even computers can be used as collateral. The equipment must have a firm resale value. Obsolete, rare or unusual equipment cannot be used as collateral.

After appraisal by an independent party, the company begins to work out the loan terms, which depend principally on the expected useful life of the equipment and the financial condition of the borrower. Frequently, a company can arrange a loan to cover even a down payment on some new equipment.

- **Receivable loans.** For a time, banks were taking on a growing portion of receivables financing. With tighter credit conditions, more recent receivables-financing activity tends to be concentrated in commercial finance companies. Relatively young receivables accounts from creditworthy customers qualify for loans. You are charged interest only on the amount due.

➤ **Observation:** Most asset-based financing companies have minimum loan provisions, usually of about $100,000. The more you borrow, the more favorable the rate. Be prepared to guarantee the loan personally: A personal guarantee is a requirement with a commercial finance company.

Using a Factor

If your company needs financing to build up inventories in advance of heavy shipping dates, or has trouble handling swollen accounts receivable after a peak season, a **factor** might be able to put your business on a more even keel.

In a factoring arrangement, your company actually sells its receivables to the factor, which then assumes all credit risks without recourse. Factoring has long been a common business practice in the textile and apparel industries, but it has been slow to spread to other industries. This is because factors have historically adopted an insular attitude, and because customers in the industries where factoring is not common are sometimes disturbed at having their accounts assigned to third parties. However, competition has heated up among factors, and many are now seeking clients outside their traditional industries.

Along with this change in attitude has come a variety of new factoring services that can be specially tailored to a variety of needs. Most factors currently provide the following services:

- **Maturity factoring.** In this traditional form of factoring, you sell the accounts receivable to the factor and you receive your money when the invoice matures (usually 30 days). The customer is notified that he or she is to forward payment directly to the factor, which handles all the collection and bookkeeping chores.
- **Nonnotification factoring.** Under this arrangement, your company handles the bookkeeping and collects payments. You get a break on the fees, and your customer doesn't have to know about the factoring arrangement.

Factoring has a big advantage over accounts-receivable loans in that you receive the full amount of your receivables as they come due, rather than the 70–80 percent that you get from a bank loan. Also, factors offer cash advances on receivables not yet due. These are essentially loans that the company uses to cover peak inventory buildups in anticipation of a bulge in receivables. Rates charged on advances usually vary between 1 percent and 3 percent over prime.

Can you use a factor? If you believe that the time, talent and resources now being directed to credit operations might be better spent on sales or production, you can probably use the services of a factor. This is particularly true if you periodically need additional cash to ease seasonal or cyclical financial obligations. Keep in mind that factoring fees are relatively high and typically run between 1 percent and 2 percent of the amount factored. Against this, however, you may be able to cut down, or even eliminate, your credit department.

It is unlikely that nonfinancial managers will get involved in more sophisticated financing maneuvers, but the following section briefly explores other financing techniques that you may encounter in your job.

Bond Financing

Bonds are actually loans that people, like you and me, make to companies. In exchange for the loan money, companies issue bonds. The terms of the loan are set out in a written agreement called the **bond indenture**. This stipulates the interest rate that will be paid to bondholders and when the principal will be repaid. It also designates a trustee, who is responsible for seeing that the terms of the agreement are met.

Illustration: A $1,000 bond may guarantee to pay 10 percent interest (often referred to as a 10 percent **coupon rate**) annually over 10 years. The interest is paid at specific times, usually every six months. At the end of the 10-year period (the **maturity date**) the company repays the investor the original $1,000 (the **principal**).

Although your firm may decide to issue bonds on its own, it's more likely that management will use an outside investment banker to underwrite the bond offering. Like stock offerings, the selling or issuing of bonds is heavily regulated by the Securities and Exchange Commission, which requires a company to meet a number of legal requirements. Thus, it's often much easier for a company to turn the "floating" of bonds over to a professional investment banker, especially if it's the first time your firm is going into the bond market.

An investment banker buys the company's bond issue and then resells it to the public; it absorbs the loss if there are any bonds that it cannot resell. For its services, the investment banker receives a fee. Keep in mind that bond interest is paid from pretax dollars, and that bondholders are creditors of your firm.

There are all sorts of bonds, but here are a few of the more common types:

- **Mortgage bonds.** As the name indicates, the company pledges as collateral specific fixed assets, such as a building. Generally, the asset is of greater value than the value of the bonds issued. This ensures that, in case of a bond default, the investors have sufficient financial protection through resale of the asset.
- **Collateral trust bonds.** In this variation of mortgage bonds, the assets used as collateral are stocks and bonds of other companies in which your firm holds an interest.
- **Equipment trust certificates.** This type of financing is favored by railroads and airlines to make major equipment purchases. The company sells the certificates to investors, and the proceeds are used to pay for the equipment, such as railroad cars or airplanes. The trustee takes title to the equipment. The railroad or airline then pays the periodic interest and the principal to the investors over a period of time, say 15 years. When all the certificates are finally paid off, title passes from the trustee to the airline or railroad.
- **Debentures.** These are, in effect, unsecured bonds. As an issuing company, you simply promise to pay interest on the debenture and repay it in the same way you would a bond, except that you don't pledge any assets. Because there isn't any collateral, investors assume a greater risk and require a higher interest rate than they would on a secured bond.

In another variation, your company may want to add a bit of incentive to investors by making your bonds and debentures **convertible**. This means the purchaser of your convertible bonds or debentures has the option of exchanging them for a specified number of shares of your common stock. The attraction here is that the price of your stock may increase, so it pays the investor to convert to stock. If this occurs, your company no longer has to pay interest or the principal.

Your company may employ other factors that are attractive to the prospective bondholder, as well as your company. For example, the company may develop a **sinking fund**, which means the firm sets aside specified amounts to provide for the gradual retirement (repurchase) of part of the bond issue. This provides added protection for bondholders because reducing the amount of outstanding bonds lessens the risk of a default.

A company can also include a **call** feature for greater financing flexibility. This simply means that the company reserves the right to buy back the bond at a specified date before the bond falls due. The call price is greater than the principal amount and generally decreases as the bond approaches its maturity date. Companies can exercise the call feature, for example, when market interest rates drop, allowing the firm to repay the bondholder and then refinance at a lower interest rate. Although the call feature is attractive for the company, it's not an advantage for the bondholder because he or she is giving up the higher interest payments of the bond. As a partial remedy, bonds with call features typically carry a higher interest rate.

Raising Equity Capital

Equity capital enjoys only one significant advantage over borrowed capital, but for some this advantage outweighs all the other drawbacks: Equity capital is permanent capital; it need not ever be repaid.

However, whenever your company accepts this permanent capital, it will, in effect, also be accepting a partner who will share in the fortunes of the firm from thereon. Therefore, before management decides that the equity market is a good idea, it should first answer a fundamental question: Is the permanent nature of the new capital that will be raised worth the dilution of control that may go with it?

There are four distinct financing methods. Management can (1) seek out a venture capitalist; (2) raise the money through private investors; (3) try private placement through an institution or investment bankers; or (4) plan a public offering. For the nonfinancial manager who is considering starting a business of her own, the second section is particularly important: Private investment funds have been the source of money for hundreds of successful start-ups.

How to Attract a Venture Capitalist

The first way to raise equity capital is through a **venture capitalist**, who invests in new companies. The best way to attract a venture capitalist is to have a "friend in court." If you know someone who has had dealings with a venture capitalist, his introduction will help. Still, a recent survey indicated that well over 80 percent of all venture capital firms have no particular preference on how they are approached.

Holding the attention of a venture capitalist might be another matter, however. Venture capital firms maintain strict investment standards. They require the same information as a banker would—and more. If you are interested in establishing such a relationship, here are ways to improve the odds:

1. **Growth.** Be ready to demonstrate how you can increase your revenue by about $15 million and/or your profits by $1 million within the next three to five years. Otherwise, venture capitalists are unlikely to show much interest.
2. **Product line.** Most venture capital firms concentrate on industries in which they have acquired a certain amount of expertise, or those that promise unusual growth. If you can locate a venture capital firm that knows your industry, your chances will significantly improve.
3. **Your management team.** Venture capitalists tend to avoid a "one-man show," no matter how exciting the prospects may be. Firms that can demonstrate management capability in a

number of areas, such as finance, marketing, production and administration, generally receive preferential treatment.

4. **Long-term planning.** It's essential that you draw up a sound corporate plan for at least five years, including cash-flow and income assumptions, before discussions with a venture capitalist begin. Give some thought to eventual corporate goals, such as public ownership, a merger or other possibilities that will enable the venture capitalist to withdraw from the firm in five to seven years.

➤ **Observation:** If your firm doesn't meet the standards discussed above, you will probably be wasting your time trying to court a venture capitalist. Although funding has increased dramatically in the past several years, venture capitalists still accept only about 5 percent of the deals offered to them.

Evaluating a Venture Capitalist

You can avoid an uncomfortable, time-wasting relationship with a venture capitalist by doing a little evaluating on your own. A venture capitalist may ask for up to 60 percent of your company, so the association should have concrete rewards for you. Here are some guidelines to follow in your evaluation:

- Check out how a venture capitalist's clients fared in the past.
- Determine whether the venture capitalist helps her clients with additional financing if it's necessary. You will probably need additional financing for your firm in the future if the first one is successful.
- Agree on what role—active participant or passive investor—the venture capitalist will play in your firm. You might prefer that he merely sit on the sidelines after the deal is made, or you might want active involvement in management. Whatever your wishes, make sure they coincide with those of the venture capitalist.
- Find out what kind of reputation the venture capitalist enjoys in the business community. You will want to know whether the reputation will help or hinder you in attracting other financing sources.

Dealing With an SBIC

Small business investment companies (SBICs), a specialized form of venture capital firms, have become an important source of capital. SBICs are licensed by the federal government to fill a financing gap for small business. SBICs can borrow up to four times their private capital position from the U.S. government at favorable borrowing rates. Most SBICs attempt to cover only operating expenses on loans, with profits coming from equity participation. Thus, the interest-rate spread is narrow. Often, a borrower from an SBIC pays no more than one-fourth of 1 percent over the SBIC's cost of funds. Moreover, because an SBIC does cover operating expenses on the loan portion of its portfolio, it can afford to lower its sights on expected returns from equity participations. For this reason, the terms of an equity deal with an SBIC are usually more favorable for you than would be possible with other venture capitalists. Here are a few additional details:

Length of loan. By law, the term of all SBIC loans must be between five and 15 years. As a practical matter, however, few SBIC loans are made for more than 10 years. Most SBICs prefer loans that mature in about seven years.

Equity participation. Usually, an SBIC makes a **convertible loan**, under which it reserves the right to convert the loan to common stock at specified, prenegotiated times. Amounts of common stock available for conversion and the conversion terms will, of course, depend on the size of the loan and the inherent risk in your company. In no case, however, can the SBIC assume control of a company—it's prohibited by law from doing so. As with venture capital companies, most SBICs will offer management assistance, should you need it.

Cashing in. Upon conversion, the SBIC might dispose of the stock in a number of ways, including a public offering, a private sale or possibly even selling the stock back to the company. Whatever the case, you will usually explore the alternatives thoroughly during negotiations.

➤ **Observation:** To get started with an SBIC financing, you will need a detailed business plan. Also, look around for an SBIC that has some familiarity with your industry and its problems. Finally, some SBICs prefer to concentrate only on fast-growing companies, while others are satisfied with companies growing at a more deliberate pace.

Virtually all SBICs are members of the Small Business Investor Alliance, formerly known as the National Association of Small Business Investment Companies. This organization can tell you all you want to know about SBICs, including the location of those nearest you. For more information, visit www.nasbic.org.

The Role of the Private Investor

For small, closely held firms, private investors are by far their most important source of equity capital. This equity can take a number of forms. Usually, equity capital denotes common stock, but many private financing deals involve preferred stock, debentures or even warrants that are convertible into common stock. Thus, while an ownership interest is almost always involved, it need not start out with common stock.

Don't expect a private investor to accept a passive role in the firm. They are almost always active investors looking to contribute more than capital. Usually, as part of the investment agreement, they act as consultants or serve on your board of directors. Thus, in a search for investors, managers should attempt to identify those investors with experience and skills that can contribute to the company's progress.

As a rule, investors in closely held firms are willing to accept a greater degree of risk than investors in public companies. In return, they expect to receive higher rewards. In a sense, then, you are buying capital rather than selling equity. The rewards that you are willing to grant to your investors are, in effect, your cost of capital. Therefore, the higher the risks, the greater the capital costs. Obviously, there can be no hard-and-fast rules for determining the extent of the returns you must offer to attract private investors, but there are some broad guidelines for establishing possible ranges. For instance, in a start-up situation, investors usually expect to earn about 10 times their investment in five years, a compound annual return of 60 percent per year.

Private investors in fledgling firms usually expect to earn about six times their investment in five years, a still-high annual compound return of 43 percent. A relatively young firm would have to offer private investors the chance to quadruple their money in five years to attract capital, and even an established firm would need to offer them the opportunity to triple their money in five years. That works out to compound annual returns of 38 percent and 25 percent, respectively.

➤ **Observation:** Expensive as they seem, expectations for private investors, even in high-risk, early-stage companies, are significantly lower than those for professional venture capital firms. In part, this seeming discrepancy stems from the "not-for-profit-only" characteristic of many private investors. In most instances, private investors back companies partly for noneconomic reasons, such as achieving a worthwhile social benefit, helping a friend or fulfilling a community need.

Private investors tend to be much less formal than their professional counterparts. Still, on average, they turn down two out of every three deals offered to them. You can improve your chances of making a favorable impression on private investors by following these important guidelines:

- **Be specific.** Put your proposal in writing. Don't expect to wing it simply because the potential investor is an individual or a friend, rather than an institution. Most private investors require a well-defined business plan. Even where a business plan is not necessary, you should draw up a well-thought-out financing proposal.
- **Be realistic.** This includes an objective appraisal of the prospects and problems facing your company, and the risks and potential rewards in the investment itself. Any attempt to minimize risks or problems will almost certainly cause the investor to back off.
- **Discuss your management team.** In reviewing a small company, nothing is more impressive to a potential investor than a dedicated, competent management team. Make sure you demonstrate that to potential investors.

The primary reason for the increased risk incurred by a private investor is the lack of liquidity in the investment. In other words, it can be difficult to find a buyer for the stock of a closely held firm, particularly for a minority interest in that firm. Therefore, you will probably need to offer an exit formula. Usually, this involves the right to tender the stock to the company at a specified date and at a price related to book value, cash flow or earnings. Another common exit formula sets aside an agreed-on percentage of earnings to purchase a segment of securities held by the investor at a prearranged price.

➤ **Observation:** When negotiating an exit formula, remember that private investors normally have much longer time horizons than the three to five years favored by venture capitalists. One recent poll disclosed that nearly 25 percent of all private investors either had no time preference or expected to hold their investments for more than 10 years.

How do you find a suitable private investor? This can be a thorny problem: There isn't exactly a referral service geared toward putting potential private investors in touch with companies seeking equity capital. To locate prospective investors, you will be forced to build your own network.

Your most fruitful source of information will probably be your friends and business associates. Investment bankers are another common source. Your other professional advisers, such as accountants, lawyers and bankers, may be helpful. Finally, be sure to investigate any venture capital clubs in your area, as well as business and community associations. (*Note:* Venture capital clubs are groups of individual investors, and should not be confused with venture capital firms.) Community associations can be particularly important because private investors tend to concentrate on companies in their geographic areas so that they can maintain close contact with their investment.

Regulation D Private Placement

Small and midsize companies are increasingly using private placements as fund-raising vehicles, thanks to a 1982 streamlining of the rules known as Regulation D. In a private placement, stocks or bonds are sold directly to an institutional investor or a small group of institutional investors.

Regulation D is specifically directed toward opening up the huge private placement market. In several ways, the regulation can help a small business raise capital through a private placement. First, Regulation D increases the amount of capital that can be raised under various categories. Under the smallest classification (Rule 504), you can raise $500,000 in 12 months versus $100,000 under the former rule. A middle category, dubbed Rule 505, allows you to raise $5 million in 12 months compared with a previous limit of $2 million in six months. In addition, there is an unlimited category dubbed Rule 506.

Second, paperwork has been cut drastically. There are no specific disclosure requirements under Rule 504. You need to comply only with antifraud provisions. This essentially means that you must give investors an accurate picture of your company with no material omissions in your offering memorandum.

Third, under Rule 504 you can choose from an unlimited number of investors. Previous regulations placed a limit of 100 investors per offering.

Finally, to stimulate activity, Regulation D allows broker-dealers to charge a commission for helping arrange private placements. Even with the commission ruling, expenses for Regulation D offerings in the past have run from 1 percent to 5 percent. That's well below the 13 percent commonly associated with public stock offerings.

How much help will you need for private placements? If you're considering private placement, talk to your lawyer first. He can bring you up to date on your state's filing requirements, which may or may not be as liberal as the SEC's rules. If you have access to capital sources in your area, you can probably arrange your private placement without engaging the services of a broker-dealer. By all indications, a large portion of Rule 504 offerings are completed without the services of a broker. In most cases, the offering company's lawyer or accountant acts as an intermediary.

If you're considering raising funds in the private placement market, insurers are an excellent source of capital. These companies are increasingly active in working with small businesses. Regional insurers sometimes loan amounts as low as $250,000.

There are many potential advantages to working with insurance companies:

- **Potential for lower rates.** Insurers are interested primarily in long-term arrangements. Almost all speak of "relationship financing," which refers to recurring deals between a company and the insurer over many years, rather than a one-shot deal.

Therefore, they are inclined to be less concerned with short-term interest trends than are many bankers. This means insurance firms will often grant clients more favorable terms on short- and medium-term loans if this will help them nail down long-term business.

- **Flexibility.** Insurance companies will arrange straight loans, equity financing or the hybrid deals (debt plus equity financing) that have become popular recently. Keep in mind, though, that all insurance companies conduct their own credit checks. Most will consider deals only if the finances of the potential customer are regarded as "investment grade" (BBB or better) by a rating service. This means that your finances must be in good shape.

➤ **Observation:** If there is a disadvantage to working with an insurance company, it's finding the right fit between your company's financing needs and the insurance company's investment policy. Some insurers, for example, specialize in certain industries. Some require an introduction through an adviser, such as an investment banker. Every insurance company's investment strategy is unique to some degree, so you may have to do some hunting. Yet the search can be worthwhile. Look to the major insurance companies for this type of financing, such as Nationwide, Prudential, Aetna Life and Casualty, Transamerica and Travelers.

Raising Capital Through a Public Stock Offering

A public stock offering is probably the most complicated of the four ways to raise equity capital. Using this method means generating scads of paperwork to satisfy SEC rules. With that in mind, here are capsule descriptions of the four types of public stock registration open to your company:

S-1 offerings. This is the general filing registration required by the SEC and is rarely suitable for smaller companies. It requires maximum disclosure for both the offering and later statements. This can be extremely demanding and costly.

➤ **Recommendation:** S-1 registrations should be used only by larger companies that have the financial resources and the staff to complete the forms involved. The reason is very simple: S-1 registrations can cost upwards of $300,000, putting them out of reach of most small companies.

S-2 offerings. In essence, this is an S-1 offering designed for companies with a limited history: that is, no substantial sales and earnings for the past five years. For such firms, the SEC requires publishing detailed information on the use of the proceeds and issuing voluminous reports on the credibility and integrity of the principals.

S-18 offerings. The S-18 offering is geared toward small businesses that need to raise substantial amounts of money (up to $5 million). The key is that S-18 offerings are processed by regional SEC offices, and there is no need to file with the SEC's Washington headquarters. This cuts down the cost significantly. S-18s can be brought to market for $100,000 or less. Criteria for an S-18 offering include: (1) the offering must be for cash; (2) the company must be incorporated in the United States or Canada; and (3) the firm may not be an investment company or limited partnership.

Regulation A offerings. This type is designed specifically for small companies and is exempt from many of the filing requirements. To qualify, your company cannot have more than $1 million in assets or 500 shareholders. No more than $1.5 million can be raised. Sometimes Regulation A offerings can be brought to market for as little as $50,000.

➤ **Observation:** The filing of a registration statement for a new public common stock offering involves a great deal of red tape, with the costs borne by the company. Some of the individual costs involved are as follows: the time managers must devote to preparing a prospectus; your own lawyer's and the underwriter's lawyer's fees; printing costs, including the prospectus and registration statement; registration costs for every state in which the stock is to be sold; accounting fees; SEC fees; registration and transfer fees; and federal issue and transfer taxes (if any).

Add to these items the selling commission, and the total cost becomes significant. A recent survey indicates that the cost of floating a common stock issue amounted, on average, to nearly 13 percent of the proceeds. Keep in mind that this is for an average offering. Without economies of scale, costs for smaller offerings run relatively higher.

Other Methods of Financing

In addition to the more traditional ways of raising capital through bank loans or stock and bond offerings, there are a number of lesser-known methods, many of which are simply variations of the traditional ones.

A Look at Leasing

By definition, you may wonder how leasing could be included in a discussion on sources of financing. After all, a lease is an agreement (contract) conveying to a business (the lessee) the right to use specified property, plant or equipment owned by another party (the lessor) for a stated period of time.

Although leasing may not technically be a source of capital, it does make additional capital available to a company by permitting the firm to finance 100 percent of the acquisition cost of an asset, whereas a typical equipment loan may require a 20 percent to 30 percent down payment. Similarly, delivery and installation charges, certain taxes, insurance, legal and clerical costs of arranging the lease, and maintenance expenses are among the other cost elements that may be incorporated into the rental installments and thus financed over the lease term.

Even though the Tax Reform Act of 1986 increased the after-tax cost of leasing, it is still one of the few potential sources of no-money-down, fixed-rate financing. It conserves cash and on-the-book borrowing capacity (because leases are not recorded as a liability on the balance sheet), and it transfers some of the risks of equipment obsolescence to the lessor. Companies with heavy debt burdens—often from leveraged buyouts—are turning increasingly to leasing as a way to finance new equipment.

Although the tax act may have increased the costs, there are two key factors that many companies still aren't considering in their buy-versus-lease decision making:

- **The repeal of the investment tax credit** and the lengthening of depreciation schedules for some equipment have increased the cost of buying more than they have the cost of leasing in many cases. Lease on a case-by-case basis.
- **The act established the alternative minimum tax (AMT),** which imposes a 20 percent tax on many common tax deductions designated as "tax preference items." The idea was to make sure companies couldn't have so many deductions that they would end up paying no taxes.

What is significant in the leasing arena is that accelerated depreciation—a big reason in the past for buying an asset—is among those tax preference items. However, if your company is subject to AMT and it leases, you can deduct the rent or lease payments as expenses for both regular tax and AMT purposes.

Don't Forget Development Corporations

What about those LDCs, CDCs and BDOs? In each case, the *D* in the middle stands for "development." Originally, these organizations were formed to act as a clearinghouse, matching a company in need of funds with a potential investor. Some now go a bit further, but community development remains their chief aim. Here's a brief look at each one:

Local development corporations (LDCs). Usually, an LDC is a privately sponsored community agency that brings together businesses and sources of capital. Generally, it is staffed by volunteers and is a nonprofit agency. Some LDCs borrow from the SBA to relend the money to a qualified small business. In some states, state funding is available.

Community development corporations (CDCs). Unlike LDCs, which function largely on an informal basis, CDCs usually operate with a permanent, full-time staff. They provide venture capital or secured financing to eligible companies willing to relocate to their area. Most CDCs are nonprofit and receive funding from state agencies and private sources.

Business development organizations (BDOs). These were conceived as a sort of packaging center where a business (particularly in a minority neighborhood) could be put in touch with local banks or government officials. They also help prepare business plans, financial statements and loan applications.

➤ **Observation:** Most states have some sort of program designed to attract and aid businesses, especially small companies. These programs vary greatly from state to state, and space precludes discussion of them all. You can obtain a free booklet describing the various state programs by contacting the SBA office nearest you.

Glossary

Accounting equation: Assets = liabilities + stockholders' equity.

Accounts payable: Money that a company owes its vendors and suppliers.

Accounts receivable: Money that customers owe a company.

Accrual accounting: An accounting method that recognizes revenue/expense transactions when they occur, not necessarily when cash is received or paid out.

Amortization: A process of writing off assets over a fixed period.

Assets: Resources that a company owns.

Audit: A look at a company's records and financial statements to ensure their accuracy.

Balance: The dollar amount of an account at a specific point in time.

Balance sheet: A statement on a firm's financial position at a particular point in time; uses the ingredients of the accounting equation: assets, liabilities and equity.

Bond: A debt instrument sold to investors and promising to return the principal and pay a stated rate of interest at specific times.

Book value: The historical cost of an asset, less any accumulated depreciation. In terms of stock, book value of a common share is the company's net worth minus the value of preferred stock, divided by the number of common shares outstanding.

Break-even: The point in a business where sales income or revenue equals expenses.

Budget: A company's written plan outlining its spending goals.

Capital budget: An analysis of long-term projects for their risk and profitability.

Capital expenditure: A purchase of a major asset, or an investment.

Cash: Bills, coins and demand deposits, such as checking accounts.

Cash accounting: An accounting method in which a transaction is recorded when cash is actually received or paid out.

Cash budget: A plan for cash receipts and expenditures during a given period.

Cash flow: The difference between cash receipts and cash disbursements. Also defined as net income plus depreciation.

Collateral: The assets a company puts up or pledges as security on a loan.

Collateral trust bond: A bond in which the issuer uses the stocks and bonds of other companies as collateral.

Commercial paper: Unsecured promissory notes generally floated by large companies to fill short-term cash needs.

Common stock: A security issued by a company to obtain capital. Holders of such securities are part owners and may or may not receive dividends.

Convertible securities: Any type of bond, note, debenture or preferred stock that can be converted to common stock.

Cost: The value of something that was given up to acquire an item.

Cost accounting: The amassing of information for reporting the costs incurred in the production of products or services.

Cost of capital: The rate of return a company must offer to obtain borrowed or invested funds.

Cost of goods sold: The amounts paid for the purchased materials, components and finished products; direct payroll; operating overhead; and other costs of acquiring or producing the products or services sold.

Cost per unit: The average cost of production for a particular volume of production.

Credit (CR): An accounting entry that increases a liability and revenue; decreases an asset and an expense.

Current assets: All cash held (primarily in bank balances or money market funds); resources that will be converted to cash in the normal course of business within one business year; plus other resources that could or will be converted within a year (marketable securities, etc.).

Current liabilities: Outstanding trade debts and obligations (trade accounts payable, short-term notes payable, current installments due on long-term debts, etc.) that will fall due in the course of normal business within a year.

Current ratio: Total current assets, divided by total current liabilities at the same point in time. Indicates the liquidity of a company.

Days sales outstanding (DSO): This represents the average collection period for accounts receivable. It's calculated as receivables multiplied by 365, divided by annual credit sales.

Debenture: An unsecured bond, or a bond for which a company doesn't pledge any of its assets.

Debit (DR): An accounting entry that increases an asset and expense; decreases a liability and revenue.

Debt/equity ratio: Total current and long-term liabilities divided by average shareholders' equity.

Deferred income taxes: That portion of a company's current tax expense that will be paid at some unstated time in the future.

Depreciation: The conversion of a fixed asset to an expense over a period of years. Although charged against income for tax calculation purposes, it involves no actual outlay of cash.

Discounted cash flow (DCF): A process to determine what a future cash flow is worth today. Used in calculating net present value and internal rate of return.

Dividend: Money or stock periodically paid to shareholders in return for their investment in a company.

Earnings per share: Earnings available to common shareholders on a per-share basis. It's calculated as net income minus preferred-stock dividends, divided by number of common shares outstanding.

Equipment trust certificate: A debt instrument offered to investors to finance the purchase of equipment, such as railroad cars or airplanes.

Equity: The amount of investment that owners or shareholders have in a company. Also called net worth. (Assets – Liabilities = Equity)

Equity turnover: Net sales divided by average shareholders' equity for the period.

Factoring: The sale of a company's receivables to a third party, called a factor, "without recourse" (that is, the factor accepts all bad-debt risks).

Finished goods: Products ready for sale.

Fiscal year: The annual time period that a company picks to report on its operation. This is generally the calendar year.

Fixed assets: All property, plants and equipment (buildings, real estate, machines, furniture, etc.) used in a business.

Fixed-asset turnover: Net sales divided by gross plant and equipment (before depreciation deduction) for the period.

Fixed costs: These are company costs that don't change as sales activity moves up or down. Essentially, they're regarded as overhead.

Goodwill: Amount paid in excess of the market value of a company's specific tangible assets.

Gross profit: The difference between net sales or revenues and the cost of the products or services sold.

Gross sales/revenues: The actual total dollars billed for goods sold or services provided, before returns, discounts and allowances granted.

Historical cost: The original amount paid to acquire an asset.

Hurdle rate: The minimum acceptable rate of return on an investment.

Income statement: The summary of a company's revenues and expenses for a particular accounting period, such as a month, quarter or year.

Indenture: An agreement containing the terms and conditions of a bond offering.

Intangible assets: Those resources of a company that don't have physical form.

Internal rate of return (IRR): A method that finds the specific percentage of a return by discounting cash flows until they reach a net present value of zero.

Inventory: Stocks of goods held for use in production, or for sale or resale by a company.

Investment banker: A company that buys a firm's securities and resells them to the public. The investment banker underwrites a bond or stock issue (that is, absorbs the loss for any part of the issue it cannot resell to the public).

Investment tax credit (ITC): A reduction in a company's tax liability resulting from the acquisition of certain equipment.

Joint venture: Formation of a partnership or corporation to carry out a particular project.

Journal: A record of a company's financial transactions kept in chronological sequence.

Ledger: A record of a company's financial transactions as they affect each account.

Leverage: A measure of a company's indebtedness. A highly leveraged firm is one that has done a large amount of borrowing or contains a good deal of debt in proportion to its equity.

Liabilities: The financial obligations that a firm has to outside creditors.

Line of credit: The maximum number of dollars a company or a bank permits a customer or firm to owe at any one time.

Liquidity: A measure of the amount of resources a company has that are cash or can be converted to cash in the near term to pay its bills on time.

Loan agreement: A written statement containing the terms and conditions of a loan.

Long-term debt: A debt that is scheduled to mature more than a year from the present time.

Marginal income: The amount realized after subtracting the cost per unit from the price per unit.

Market price: The amount of money a share of stock is worth on a stock exchange, the over-the-counter market or to an individual buyer.

Marketable securities: Securities, such as stocks or bonds, that can be easily sold.

Mortgage bond: A bond for which the issuer pledges certain fixed assets, such as a building, as collateral.

Net income (profit) after taxes: The final "bottom-line" profit cleared by the business from all sources.

Net operating profit: Gross profit, less selling costs and administrative overhead.

Net present value (NPV): A method of evaluating an investment by converting future cash inflows and outflows to their present value through the use of present value tables.

Nonoperating expenses: Interest paid on long-term debts, losses on sales of capital assets, etc.

Nonoperating income: Interest and dividends received on investments, gains on the disposition of capital assets, etc.

Operating budget: A budget that includes the sales, expense and production budgets of a company. It provides all the information necessary to produce a pro forma (projected) income statement.

Operating margin: The percentage derived when operating income is divided by sales, giving you a profitability ratio.

Outstanding shares: Shares issued by a company and owned by shareholders.

Par value: The nominal or face value of stocks and bonds at the time of issuance.

Partnership: An unincorporated business owned by two or more persons who are personally responsible for all the business' debts.

Payback: A method that estimates the time it will take to receive enough cash from a project to recover the cash invested in that project.

Preferred stock: A share in a company that usually carries a fixed dividend and entitles its owner to payment prior to that of a common shareholder in the event of bankruptcy.

Private placement: The sale of a company's securities to an institutional investor or group of institutional investors, rather than offering them to the public.

Pro forma statement: A projected or budgeted financial statement.

Profit-and-loss (P&L) statement: *See* **Income statement**. Also called earnings report.

Profit margin: The percentage derived when net income is divided by net sales. Also called return on sales (ROS).

Proprietorship: The unincorporated business of a single owner.

Raw materials: Purchased components that go into making a product.

Receivables turnover: Credit sales divided by average accounts receivable for a period.

Retained earnings: The profits a firm earned during its existence that have not been distributed to the stockholders as dividends, but kept in the firm.

Return on assets (ROA): Net operating profit for the period divided by average total tangible assets for the period.

Return on equity (ROE): Net profit for the period, divided by average shareholders' equity for the period.

Return on investment (ROI): A general term to describe a group of ratios (ROA, ROE, ROS) that measure a company's profitability.

Return on sales (ROS): *See* **Profit margin**.

Shareholders' (stockholders') equity: The par value of the corporation's common and preferred stock, plus any paid-in or accumulated capital surplus over the par value, plus any earned surplus or earnings retained for use in business. (Equity = Assets – Liabilities)

Sinking fund: Money set aside by a company to repurchase part of a bond issue.

Small business investment companies (SBICs): Specialized venture capital firms licensed and partly financed by the federal government to fill a financing gap for small firms.

Statement of cash flows: The presentation of a company's cash receipts and payments over a period of time.

Tangible assets: Those resources of a company that have physical form, such as a building or plant.

Treasury stock: Shares a company owns through the repurchase of the stock from shareholders.

Trial balance: A comparison of the totals of debit columns for all accounts with the credit columns for all accounts. They should balance.

Variable costs: Costs that directly depend on sales activity.

Variance: The difference between expected or budgeted results and actual results.

Venture capital: Funds that a person or company willing to take a risk invests in a small business.

Work-in-process: Goods on which production has begun, but which have not yet been finished.

Working capital: Current assets less current liabilities.

Zero-base budgeting (ZBB): A budgeting process in which department heads or managers must justify all expense plans and rank them based on their overall contribution to the company.

MANAGEMENT RESOURCES FOR SUCCESS

- **Manage difficult personality types**
- **Negotiate to get what you want**
- **Win at office politics**
- **Conduct effective performance reviews**
- **Maximize productivity**

BusinessManagement DAILY

About Business Management Daily

Business Management Daily (BMD) was founded in 1987 to provide timely business and career advice to professionals.

Since that time, BMD has grown to become America's leading advisor on the trends, laws and situations that affect decision-makers in the workplace.

We provide reliable advice that business people can apply in real-world situations. We help people across all industries save on taxes, avoid lawsuits, recruit the best talent, become better leaders and more.

Visit www.BusinessManagementDaily.com to learn about all of our products and services.

BusinessManagement DAILY

Business Management Daily
7600A Leesburg Pike • West Building, Suite 300
Falls Church, VA 22043-2004
Phone: (800) 543-2055 8:30 am–6 pm, ET
Fax: (703) 905-8040
Web: www.BusinessManagementDaily.com
Email: customer@BusinessManagementDaily.com

NIBM-BR-MGT

PLEASE RUSH THESE RESOURCES!

☐ **Manager's Guide to Effective, Legal Performance Reviews**
$39.95 (BEPR)

☐ **Mastering Business Negotiation**
$39.95 (BMBN)

☐ **Mastering Office Politics**
$39.95 (BMOP)

☐ **Mastering Business Presentations**
$39.95 (BMBP)

☐ **The Truth About Leadership**
$39.95 (BTAL)

☐ **The Manager's Handbook: 104 Solutions to Your Everyday Workplace Problems**
$59.95 (BMHB)

☐ **Difficult People at Work**
$39.95 (BDPW)

☐ **Control the Chaos**
$39.95 (BCCM)

☐ **Mastering Business Etiquette & Protocol**
$39.95 (BMBE)

☐ **Mastering Business Finance**
$39.95 (BMBF)

Special Offer Code Y11304

VA residents add 5% sales tax.

SHIPPING & HANDLING
• • • • •
$6.00 for each item;

Book subtotal: _____
Add s&h (below): _____
TOTAL: _____

MONEY-BACK GUARANTEE
+++ 100% +++

FOR FASTER SERVICE, CALL (800) 543-2055

☐ CHECK ENCLOSED (payable to: Business Management Daily) **OR**

CHARGE MY: ☐ VISA ☐ MC ☐ AMEX ☐ DISC

ACCT. # _____ EXPIRES _____

SIGNATURE _____

NAME _____

COMPANY _____

ADDRESS _____

CITY _____ STATE ____ ZIP ____

TEL. _____ EMAIL _____

DETACH & MAIL WITH PAYMENT TO:
Business Management Daily
7600A Leesburg Pike, West Building, Suite 300
Falls Church, VA 22043-2004
OR FAX CREDIT CARD ORDERS TO: (703) 905-8040

Mastering Business Presentations

Walk into any spotlight knowing that you'll walk out a winner! No matter where or when you're giving a presentation, you'll be cool, clear and persuasive with tactics that make your points come alive, distill your best message and mellow the toughest audience. Use the methods perfected by legendary speakers such as FDR and Abraham Lincoln and by high-profilers Steve Jobs and Jerry Seinfeld. Then enjoy the applause!

$39.95 68 pages

The Truth About Leadership

Reveal your hidden leadership abilities and spur your team to victory. Learn that elusive ability to unite individuals and propel your organization beyond all expectations. Boost your leadership abilities by discovering how to lead through a crisis, the best ways to take on a titan, the right time to burn bridges and much more!

$39.95 65 pages

BEST-SELLER

The Manager's Handbook: 104 Solutions to Your Everyday Workplace Problems

The biggest challenge for managers? Managing your own workload. At last, there's one resource that helps you do everything better. *The Manager's Handbook: 104 Solutions to Your Everyday Workplace Problems* will help you manage better from day one. No lofty theories or buzzwords—just practical advice that helps you get the job done while staying out of legal trouble. This generous handbook is nearly 200 pages long—198, to be exact. Plus it has a generous table of contents to make it easy to find exactly what you need. Solve problems, hire, fire, coach and review employees with confidence.

$59.95 198 pages

Mastering Business Etiquette & Protocol

This invaluable report reveals the critical connection between protocol and profit, something most people forget, neglect or just never get around to learning in the first place. Discover the how-to of it all, including making proper introductions, writing effective letters, winning back disgruntled customers, handling meetings and special events properly, and much more!

$39.95 40 pages

Mastering Business Finance

Learn how to crunch the numbers like a Wall Street pro! If you want security and job advancement, you need to understand the numbers that drive your company. Use this guide to strip away the intimidation surrounding a complex subject.

$39.95 92 pages

Mastering Business Negotiation

This step-by-step guide is for anyone (even the pushy, impulsive or tongue-tied) who wants a better deal at work, at home and in life! You'll get pointers to build skills in four critical areas and learn to negotiate with forcefulness and grace.

$39.95 84 pages

Mastering Office Politics

How often have you heard that the only way to win at office politics is with dirty tricks? It's really about subtlety, finesse and the artful orchestration of your agenda. This special report contains six sections: advancement, roadblocks, teamwork, leadership, change and managing difficult employees ... each is an instant how-to guide for almost any conceivable political situation.

$39.95 116 pages

MANAGEMENT RESOURCES FOR SUCCESS

Business Management Daily has compiled this collection of resources to help you handle some of the most challenging situations you may face in the workplace.

From dealing with office politics and difficult people to giving performance appraisals that are legal and motivating, we have the do's and don'ts!

BEST-SELLER

Manager's Guide to Effective, Legal Performance Reviews

Make your performance appraisals work for you, not against you! How you conduct an employee's performance review can have a major impact on how that employee behaves. Many books offer general suggestions for improving performance, but few discuss specific ways to make reviews more effective. *Effective, Legal Performance Reviews* shows you how to conduct appraisals with clearly established expectations and no misinterpretation.

$39.95 90 pages

Difficult People at Work

Working with underhanded, self-centered troublemakers is infuriating. This special report will teach you to identify and manage the 24 most challenging personality types and give you proven strategies to put problem people in their place.

$39.95 42 pages

Control the Chaos

Discover field-proven techniques that make it possible for you to leave work every day with a feeling of accomplishment, and improve your reputation with upper management, despite working fewer hours!

$39.95 36 pages

43749577R00057

Made in the USA
Middletown, DE
18 May 2017